ASSASSINATION
OF THE AMERICAN
CHARACTER

WHERE ARE THE HEROES?

CHARLES BROWN

PAGE PUBLISHING
Conneaut Lake, PA

First originally published by Page Publishing 2023

ISBN 979-8-88793-101-2 (pbk)
ISBN 979-8-88793-102-9 (digital)

Printed in the United States of America

If we lived in a state where virtue was profitable, common sense would make us saintly. But since we see that avarice, anger, pride, and stupidity commonly profit far beyond charity, modesty, justice, and thought perhaps we must stand fast a little, even at the risk of being heroes.
—Thomas More, *A Man for All Seasons*

And he shall be like a tree planted by the rivers of water, that bringeth forth his fruit in his season; his leaf also shall not wither; and whatsoever he doeth shall prosper.
—Psalm 1:3

ACKNOWLEDGMENTS

My heroes are my close friends, Vladyslava Kalandyrits and Charles Drake. They have provided moral, spiritual, and monetary support along the way. Their faith in me was the driving force behind the completion of this book. May God bless them.

I would also like to include my grandson, Brendon Michael Sullivan, who has been with me from the beginning and has always been supportive.

PREFACE

— ∞ —

Theological priorities: What should they be and why?

No apology here. In all of human history, God is the ultimate authority. As James Madison stated, "If men were angels no government would be necessary." When the American character retains its godliness, we, many times, get the leaders we need and deserve. With the absence of God in our daily lives, we get the leaders we deserve, not who we need. But too often, due to human frailty, we, humans, seem to forget that God is the ultimate authority and the only authority. He is total truth. When that happens, God works into the significant history which exists. As a holy and loving God, He works in history on the basis of His character; and when His people and their culture turn away, He works in history in judgment.

In the past, I have been criticized for condemning the political objectives of our former president. I criticized him long before he was president for the associations with William Ayers and the Reverend Jeremiah Wright and the church that he pastored. I read his own autobiography, *Dreams from My Father: A Story of Race and Inheritance*, in which with his new all-Black identity, Obama stews about injustices that he never personally experienced and feeds his warped worldview by withdrawing into a "smaller and smaller coil of rage." He lives with a *nightmare vision* of Black powerlessness.

Obama says that the hate doesn't go away. "It formed a counter-narrative buried deep within each person and at the center of which stood white people—some cruel, some ignorant, sometimes a single face, sometimes just a faceless image of a system claiming power over our lives." No matter how much of this hatred was influenced by his father and others, it was further learned at the church he chose to attend for twenty years. That is the church in Chicago headed by the Reverend Jeremiah Wright.

Obama's worldview sees United States history as a consistent tale of oppressors and oppressed. He objects to the public schools because Black kids are learning "someone else's history, someone else's culture." These are all quotes from the book, his autobiography.

He sat in that church for twenty years and then claimed that he never heard the hate being preached by his pastor. It is the single most destructive element of politically correct America to fail to see and to recognize evil in the world. The leadership in our churches no longer speaks of evil; they ignore their responsibility through *moral relativism* and *moral equivalency*. They tell us that we are all sinners, which is very true; therefore, we cannot point out the evil in our culture. But evil exists and, as Christians, we must take a stand against it. We are locked in a daily, deadly battle between good and evil. A quote from Robert Bolt's play *A Man for all Seasons* defines this dilemma in a unique fashion: "If we lived in a state where virtue was profitable, common sense would make us saintly. But since we see that avarice, anger, pride, and stupidity commonly profit far beyond charity, modesty, justice, and thought perhaps we must stand fast a little, even at the risk of being heroes."

By removing the absolutes, *progressivism* and/or *liberalism* has led to a reversal of human norms and natural law while, without knowing and with indifference, we have fallen into a wilderness of *moral relativism* and *moral equivalency*.

Diversity and *moral relativism*, where no idea is superior to another, are dangerous metaphors for division, confusion, and mediocrity. Diversity is not something to strive for; it is something easily achieved if everyone strives for the truth. Democracy and the republic, as it was given to us by the Founding Fathers, is only possible among a people who believe in God and act accordingly. The conservative belief in a limited government of the people by the people and for the people is founded upon Christian principles expressed in Abraham Lincoln's second inaugural address: "With malice toward none; with charity for all; with firmness in the right, as God gives us to see the right." Where the spirit of the Lord is present, there is freedom while the alternative is tyranny. Thus tyranny becomes inevitable in a secular government.

The need for *militant Christianity* is not a supercilious notion coming from the right-wing radical nuts as the Left tends to label anyone who believes in God and is of the Christian faith, but it is in response to the drift away from any sociological, as well as theological, moorings.

Social justice agendas were launched in the name of civil rights and other rights that exist only in the minds of nine justices of the Supreme Court who were never elected to any legislative office. With the sole purpose of creating in America a cultural revolution in which God no longer dominates, the moral horizon and personal autonomy and individual choice become the twin pillars of a debased moral view. There is never any mention of equal rights requiring equal responsibility. Congress, the representatives of the people, must exercise their responsibility and their authority to reign in the excesses of the judiciary.

It is imperative that we free ourselves from the grip of Rousseau and his Enlightenment conspirators, secular humanists, who have attempted to replace our Christian attitude and strength in this country, as they have in Europe, with a system of morals and philosophy which, in the words of Winston Churchill, is "as malevolent as Christianity was benevolent, which, if not arrested would shatter irretrievably all that Christianity has rendered possible."

This malignant worldview "has been the mainspring of every subversive movement during the nineteenth century. This worldwide conspiracy for the overthrow of civilization and the reconstitution of society on the basis of arrested development, of envious malevolence, and impossible equality has been steadily growing."

Where there is a direct conflict between the laws of God and the laws of man, "We must obey God rather than men" (Acts 5:29).

We are not bound by God to follow a leader who intends to destroy this nation. We are bound by God to love all people, and Jesus tells us to love our enemies, but that does not mean that we must like or love how they think or act. President Obama has shown his disdain for Christianity with his recent mandates which are clearly in violation of the First Amendment. He intends to put our religious freedoms under the authority of the state. Our rights are endowed by our Creator, and our religious freedom is guaranteed by the constitution. Can we lose our freedoms? Yes, we can. If we refuse to take a stand against tyranny. If we refuse to obey God and follow the corrupt policies of man.

INTRODUCTION

———— ⟡ ————

Assassination of the
American Character
Unmasking the Agendas

The Search for Moral Clarity

By removing the absolutes, *progressivism* and/or *liberalism* has led to a reversal of human norms and natural law while, without knowing and with indifference, we have fallen into a wilderness of *moral relativism* and *moral equivalency.* Their goal is to destroy patriotism, morality, and spiritual life in the American mind and culture. Our idea of freedom is in danger because these three ingredients are central to the American character.

Diversity and moral relativism, where no idea is superior to another, are dangerous metaphors for division, confusion, and mediocrity. As Francis A. Schaeffer has said, "Diversity is not something to strive for; it is something easily achieved if everyone strives for the truth." Democracy is only possible among a people who believe in God. Self-government is freedom while the alternative is tyranny. Thus tyranny becomes inevitable in a secular government. It is the single most self-destructive element of politically correct America to fail to see and to recognize evil in the world. Our churches no longer speak of evil; they shirk their responsibility with *moral equivalency.* They tell us that we are all sinners and therefore cannot call out evil, but evil exists and as Christians, we are locked in the daily, deadly battle between good and evil.

The American character is the practical affirmation of God and the determination to live in the reality of His existence with the explanations in His Word. Without His Word, there is no intellectually honest basis for what is man, what gives meaning, or what are absolute morals. Without this God and man's understanding of Him, the human being will always go for substitutes: idols as visible gods, ideologies as master plans for life, personal meaning for the moment, and relative morals for personal desires. The importance of Holy Bible is clearly a vital organ of the American character. America is not now nor has it ever been a secular nation, nor has it ever been a theocracy. America has, since its conception, been a powerful religious idea, and the American character is indeed a religion in its own right; and that religion is Christianity.

We tend to see things in "bits and pieces." We see the cultural breakdown as a wide array of individual issues, family breakdown, school violence, abortion, immorality in all areas of entertainment. It is an attack on the American character by all of these agendas. It is the failure of the American character to retain its Christian belief that we are created by God in His image. As Francis Schaeffer has written, all of these forms of cultural dissolution have "come about due to a shift in worldview...a worldview based on the idea that the final reality is an impersonal matter or energy shaped into its current form by impersonal chance."

Before there was an intelligent design movement, Schaeffer saw that everything hangs on your view of origins. If you start with impersonal forces operating by chance—in other words, naturalistic evolution—then overtime, even if it takes several generations, you will end up with naturalism in moral, social, and political philosophy. Evolutionary psychology, an updated version of sociobiology, promotes the premise that if natural selection produced the human body, then it must also account for all aspects of human belief and behavior.

The ACLU and their theology of secular humanism (atheism in disguise) is attempting to gain power through the reversal of human norms, natural law, and the social institutions that are so necessary for the continuance of mankind and our republican form of government. It is a malignancy-filled system of philosophy.

The goal of all of these agendas from the left-wing liberal critique is the same. It is not the "dialectical materialism" of Marxism, for as an economic policy that is dead, yet there are those presently in the White House who are reviving the effort to destroy capitalism and the free market system with a *Cloward-Piven Strategy* of forcing political change through orchestrated crisis.

Radical organizations have been created to implement the strategy all for the purpose of creating a financial and political crisis. This strategy, as implemented in the 1960s, would actually overload the welfare system and maximize the number of people on welfare in New York City from 200,000 to 1.1 million between 1960 and 1970. Association of Community Organizations for Reform Now (ACORN), as a Saul Alinsky version of Community Organization and *Rules for Radicals*, was a major force behind the high-risk mortgage lending that eventually led to the current financial crisis.

Marxism as a social philosophy has never been more popular, and its goal is the destruction of Western civilization and in particular the American character, which is generally described as a hierarchical, heterosexual, white, Christian, patriarchal, capitalistic system of oppression. You must belong to the proper victim group or your opposition to this neo-Marxism will be properly dismissed.

G. K. Chesterton, in *The Everlasting Man*, described this reversal process as the "theology of demons" and said that it was sadistically anti-human and anti-childhood. It is intrinsically evil. It is a malignancy-filled system of philosophy posturing as something seemingly innocuous in order to infect Christendom and Christianity in the United States.

Agendas with a common link and a common purpose. That purpose being to create a society wherein the natural distinctions between male and female are dissolved. That purpose being to destroy true academic freedom by not allowing other theories except evolution to be taught to our children. That purpose being to establish an atheistic society by making law for the sake of the antichrist. That purpose being to socially indoctrinate our children and destroy our Christian heritage. That purpose being to blur the existence of God and, with His existence, the explanations in His Word. Without His Word, there is no intellectually honest basis for what is man, what gives meaning, or what are absolute morals. Without this God and man's understanding of Him, the human being will always go for substitutes: idols as visible gods, ideologies as master plans for life, personal meaning for the moment, and relative morals for personal desires. Thus creating cultural and moral anarchy. This is how this phenomenon must be viewed. This agenda-driven society controlled by evolutionary secular humanism is determined to create cultural and moral anarchy.

Each agenda is extremely well organized with specific goals and a plan of attack. The "Gay Agenda" was put forth by homosexual activists in their "1972 Gay Rights Platform." The "1972 Gay Rights Platform" reveals two of the central demands of, as Matt Barber describes them, "the homosexual lobby's lavender curtain."

One, "Repeal all laws governing the age of sexual consent." As you can see this opens up our children and teens to pedophiles and homosexuals who wish to prey on them.

Two, "Repeal all legislative provisions that restrict the sex or number of persons entering into a marriage unit." This is an all-out attempt to redefine marriage so that all objections to any conceivable combination are rendered with having no practical significance.

The idea of the American character needs to be rediscovered and strengthened and given new emphasis in a world longing for the hope of freedom. We are the result of that collective unconscious Americanism found in the American character given to us by the Puritans, by the Founding Fathers John and Samuel Adams, Jefferson, Hamilton, Madison, Elias Boudinot, and so many others that defined the American character. It is our history that the idea of America has brought a special kind of hope to the world. The agenda-driven society is attempting to extinguish that light that is the "shining city upon a hill" and this "one nation under God."

In order to understand Barack Obama, you must understand Saul Alinsky and his *Rules for Radicals*. As Jonah Goldberg points out, Alinsky's worldview is distinctly fascistic. Life is defined by war, contests of power, and the imposition of will and shares a bedrock hostility to dogma. Alinsky believes in only the desired ends of the movement, which he regards as the source of life's meaning. What comes through most is his unbridled love of power. Power is good in its own right. Ours "is a world not of angels but of angles," he proclaims in *Rules for Radicals*, "where men speak of moral principles but act on power principles."

Alinsky's method of community organizing borrowed tactics from the Catholic Church, Al Capone's mobsters, University of Chicago sociologists, and John L. Lewis's union organizers. Alinsky dedicated his book to the one that he calls the very first radical, Lucifer, "the first radical known to man who rebelled against the establishment and did it so effectively that he at least won his own kingdom."

There is a dilemma that we, in a free society, face when black and white is not clear and varying shades of gray appear to isolate the black and white. Finding moral clarity becomes far more difficult. It is very easy for those of us living in a free society to lose moral clarity. In the collective society, the primary challenge is finding the inner strength to confront evil. In the free world, the primary challenge is finding the moral clarity to see evil.

out, Alinsky's worldview is distinctly fascistic. Life is defined by war, contests of power, and the imposition of will and shares a bedrock hostility to dogma. Alinsky believes in only the desired ends of the movement, which he regards as the source of life's meaning. What comes through most is his unbridled love of power. Power is good in its own right. Ours "is a world not of angels but of angles," he proclaims in *Rules for Radicals*, "where men speak of moral principles but act on power principles."

Alinsky's method of community organizing borrowed tactics from the Catholic Church, Al Capone's mobsters, University of Chicago sociologists, and John L. Lewis's union organizers. Alinsky dedicated his book to the one that he calls the very first radical, Lucifer, "the first radical known to man who rebelled against the establishment and did it so effectively that he at least won his own kingdom."

There is a dilemma that we, in a free society, face when black and white is not clear and varying shades of gray appear to isolate the black and white. Finding moral clarity becomes far more difficult. It is very easy for those of us living in a free society to lose moral clarity. In the collective society, the primary challenge is finding the inner strength to confront evil. In the free world, the primary challenge is finding the moral clarity to see evil.

CHAPTER 1

The Faces of Publius

The *Federalist Papers* is the title given to a series of eighty-five essays, collected and edited by the American statesman Alexander Hamilton and published in two volumes in 1788. Seventy-seven of the essays had been originally published in the New York City newspaper, *The Independent Journal*, between October 17, 1787, and April 12, 1788, to refute the arguments of those opposing ratification of the proposed United States Constitution. The essays at first bore the signature "A Citizen of New York" and later the pen name "Publius." Most of them were written by Hamilton, a number were the work of the statesman James Madison, and others were written by the jurist John Jay. The authors appealed to the desire for law and order created by Shays's rebellion, contending that anarchy would ensue if the government were not centralized. They directed their most effective argument to the members of the rising commercial class, assuring them that the commerce would flourish best under the protection of a strong federal government. The essays, widely circulated in pamphlet form, were largely responsible for the ratification of the constitution by New York State in 1788.

There is little room for question or debate that the *Federalist Papers* stands third only to the Declaration of Independence and the constitution itself among all of the sacred writings of American political history.

With the Declaration of Independence, "our forefathers brought forth upon this continent a new nation, conceived in liberty." The year was 1776. From that time until May 1787, this new nation was conceived in liberty, floundered in a sea of uncertainty. The people of this new nation were beginning to realize that liberty by itself does not exist, that there is "no happiness without liberty, no liberty without self-government, no self-government without constitutionalism, no constitutionalism without morality and none of these great goods without stability and order." This was the message that Alexander Hamilton, James Madison, and John Jay hoped to convey to the people of this new nation in the *Federalist Papers*.

Delegates from the thirteen states had been invited by the existing Congress to meet in Philadelphia for the purpose of framing a new constitution. Not merely a new constitution, but one based on the concept of a strong union. Why a new constitution? Because the Articles of Confederation, under which the people were governed, had proven itself to be inadequate. There was no common interest to unite the people. The states were failing to comply with constitutional requirements. They were encroaching on federal authority and were disrupting foreign relations. They were trespassing on one another's rights and were unable to work together where their common interest required oneness. No provision existed to guarantee against internal violence, and the government could not back up laws passed by its own Congress. Some states had not even ratified the articles. Finally, the states had a tendency to pass too many laws, change them to suit themselves; ultimately many of the laws were simply unjust. These facts weighed very heavily on the delegates as they made their way to Philadelphia. The new charter of government was agreed upon and signed at Philadelphia on September 17, 1787. It was transmitted to the people of the thirteen states. Hamilton, fearing that the convention's hopes to form a more perfect union might be destroyed, set out to stiffen the support of the new constitution and instruct the minds of the people and for posterity. Thus the *Federalist Papers* was born and given its birthright under the pseudonym Publius.

Publius, the political theorist, had many faces. One face, in the person of Madison, was that of the federalist and exponent of limited government. Another face, in the person of Hamilton, was that of the nationalist and admirer of energetic government.

Underneath the different and varying facades, however, the soul of Publius was unified and searching for free government at both levels in the federal system that must exercise direct authority over individuals over a wide expanse of territory and, in the same instance, provide for the enjoyment of individual freedom. Publius, the political realist, had only one face, and that face was bound to the exposition of certain enduring truths that would provide an understanding of both the dangers of free government.

From the beginning the purpose of the *Federalist Papers* was threefold: 1) to expound and explain the blessings and the beauties of the union as a federal system; 2) to present an indictment of the Articles of Confederation for their failure to provide any semblance of good government; 3) to analyze and defend the new constitution as an instrument of federalism and constitutionalism.

The first objective of Publius was to show the American people that there was strength in unity. Externally, the new nation was left vulnerable under the articles to foreign force and influence. Internally, with no visible head of government to enforce domestic tranquility, the big states were pitted against the small states. John Jay wrote that "The number of wars which have happened or will happen in the world will always be found to be in proportion to the number and weight of the causes which provoke or invite them." If the just causes of war can be eliminated by a united America, then the union would tend most to preserve the people in a state of peace with other nations.

Internally, without the union, the rivalries of power and commerce and the desire of equality and safety would provide the causes of war among the states. Hamilton cites the balance of power struggles in Europe as an example of what would happen. Mr. Hamilton further states that the union "is a convention by which several smaller states agree to become members of a larger one, which they intend to form. It is a kind of assemblage of societies that constitute a new one, capable of increasing, by means of new associations, till they arrive to such a degree of power as to be able to provide for the security of the united body." In other words, it reconciles the advantages of monarchy with those of republicanism. Hamilton also notes the practical aspects of union as it can be utilized for the advancement of commerce and revenue and economic frugality.

Madison enters into the discourse now by noting that factions are the product and the price of liberty. He recognizes a faction as a group adverse to the rights of other citizens and states that "there are two methods of curing the mischiefs of faction: the one, by removing its cause; the other by controlling its effects." To remove the causes of faction would require the destruction of liberty, for "liberty is to faction what air is to fire, an ailment without which it instantly expires." He sees the latent causes of faction as sown in the nature of man, which leads to the conclusion that relief is to be sought only in the means of controlling its effects, and this relief is supplied by the republican principle of majority rules. However, that is not the end of the argument. In the *Federalist Papers* essay number 10, Madison comes to deal with the crucial problem of breaking or controlling the violence of faction, whether amounting to a majority or minority, by offering the crucial assumption that a broader republic with its national Congress representing many sections and groups would overcome and control the violence of faction, be it either majority or minority. Madison saw government as a necessary evil that must be curbed, not an instrument for the realization of men's higher ideals or the broader interests of the nation. "There is no maxim in my opinion which is more liable to be misapplied, and which therefore needs elucidation than the current one that the interest of the majority is the political standard of right and wrong. In fact it is only reestablishing under another name and a more specious form, force as the measure of right," stated James Madison.

Two questions emerge from all this debate. The first question is how much power does the constitution relegate to the government and what restraints does it impose on the states? The second question is how will this power be distributed among the branches of government, the legislative, the executive, and the judicial? Alexander Hamilton, in Federalist No. 81, states that "There is not a syllable in the plan under consideration which directly empowers the national courts to construe the laws according to the spirit of the constitution." To Madison, the only answer to these questions was contained in the system of checks and balances. "The great security against a gradual concentration of the several powers in the same department, consists in giving to those who administer each department the necessary constitutional means and personal motives to resist encroachments of the others, ambition must be made to counteract ambition. The interest of the man must be connected with the constitutional rights of the place." To Madison, government was the greatest of all reflections on human nature. If men were angels, no government would be necessary.

Years later, the British historian, jurist, and statesman James Bryce, Viscount Bryce (1838–1922), is best known for *The American Commonwealth*, a significant study of United States political institutions. He also fostered a revival of interest in Roman law. James Bryce, as a British statesman who served as Britain's ambassador to the United States from 1907 to 1913, Lord Bryce, as a keen observer of the American Republic and its form of government, was to note that "America is all of a piece, its institutions are a product of its economic and social conditions, an expression of its character." An expression of its character, that is to say that democracy, sound democracy and the republic, its rule by law and reliance on principles that do not change, is not a cause but an effect of our national character—character in the leaders of our institutions, both economic and social, and character in our people. Our national character will determine whether our politics is good or bad, and sometimes proudly and sometimes sadly our nation often gets the leadership it deserves when leaders devoid of character and principles are elected.

Over the years since it was published, the *Federalist Papers* has retained its high place in the sacred writings of American democracy. As a brilliant set of essays on political theory, the United States Supreme Court has, in controversial cases, often referred to the *Federalist Papers* for incisive and authoritative interpretation of the constitution. It is required reading for all Americans interested in freedom and liberty. The faith of our Founding Fathers in creating this nation under God and with God was central to their very being.

CHAPTER 2

The Dream of Religious Freedom

American Character Defined

Whenever anyone turns to the Lord, the veil is
taken away. Now the Lord is the Spirit, and where
the Spirit of the Lord is, there is freedom.
—2 Corinthians 3:16–17

Some years after the constitution had been ratified by the several States, James Bryce, a British statesman who served as Britain's ambassador to the United States from 1907 to 1913, and Lord Bryce, a keen observer of the American Republic and its form of government, was to note that "America is all of a piece, its institutions are a product of its economic and social conditions, an expression of its character." That is to say that democracy, representative democracy as it is practiced in this constitutional republic, is not a cause but an effect of our national character. The republic, its rule by law and reliance on principles that do not change, is the direct result of that uniquely American character. That unique blend of faith and freedom has been the defining feature of this nation from the beginning.

Alexis De Tocqueville was to observe that "Liberty regards religion as its companion in all its battles and its triumphs...it considers religion as the safeguard of morality, and morality as the best

security of law and the surest pledge of the duration of freedom." Since the Enlightenment of the eighteenth century, leading intellectuals have argued and held the belief that religion and politics should be separated completely, that the advance of liberty will eventually overwhelm religious beliefs, and therefore the two should be sharply divided.

Tocqueville further tells us, the more democratic the political system, the more important is religious belief: "It is more needed in democratic republics than in any others. How is it possible that society should escape destruction if the moral tie is not strengthened in proportion as the political tie is relaxed? And what can be done with a people who are their own masters if they are not submissive to the Deity?"

According to Tocqueville there is a question as to why democratic people show a more ardent and enduring love of equality than of liberty. He states, "The taste that men have for liberty and the one they feel for equality are in fact two distinct things, and I do not shrink from adding that in democratic nations they are two unequal things." He further states, "I think that democratic peoples have a natural taste for liberty. Left to themselves, they seek it out, love it, and suffer if deprived of it. For equality, however, they feel an ardent, insatiable, eternal, invincible passion. They want equality in liberty, and if they cannot have it, they want it still in slavery. They will suffer poverty, servitude, and barbarity, but they will not suffer aristocracy."

Tocqueville explains that there is a strange relationship between equality and despotism. The vices that despotism fosters are precisely those that equality encourages. They complement each other and assist each other to disastrous effect. Equality places men side by side without a common bond to hold them together. Despotism raises barriers between them to keep them apart. The former disposes them not to think of their fellowmen, and the latter makes a kind of public virtue of indifference. Despotism, dangerous at all times, makes it easy to see that at such times as these men have a particular need of liberty. "The Americans have used liberty to combat the individualism born of equality, and they have defeated it." In the final analysis, Tocqueville maintains that to combat the evils that equality may engender, there is only one effective remedy: political liberty.

Tocqueville also wrote about the application of the doctrine of self-interest properly understood in the matter of religion. He states that no matter how much mental effort is lavished on proving the usefulness of virtue, it will never be easy to make a man live well who does not wish to die. He claims that Americans adhere to their religion out of self-interest. I tend to disagree. Virtue is not always worth the effort. It has little value in today's world. If we lived in a state where virtue was profitable, common sense would elevate us to a level of sainthood. But since we see that extreme greed in search of wealth and power, anger, pride, and stupidity commonly profit far beyond charity, modesty, justice, and thought, perhaps we must stand fast a little, even at the risk of being heroes.

"I think modern people have somehow got their minds all wrong about human life. They seem to expect what Nature has never promised; and then they try to ruin all that Nature has really given. At all those atheist chapels of Ivywood they're always talking of Peace, Perfect Peace, and Utter Peace, and Universal Joy and souls that beat as one. But they don't look any more cheerful than anyone else; and the next thing they do is to start smashing a thousand good jokes and good stories and good songs and good friendships by pulling down 'The Old Ship.'"

Much of Chesterton's writing shows the conflict between Christianity and atheism. In *The Ball and the Cross* Chesterton chronicles a hot dispute between a devout but naive Roman Catholic and a zealous but naive atheist. In this case the battle is both witty and profound. Humor is the vehicle used to present a serious discussion on religious and philosophical subjects. Today, the struggle is far more serious between theism and atheism. Today it is an alliance of atheistic agendas that are attacking the American character, and their aim is to destroy that biblical republic that is the foundation of the American character.

It will always remain a dishonor, moral and intellectual dishonor, for the Western democratic societies that allowed the socialist experiments of the twentieth century to ruin the economies of whole continents and destroy the lives of countless millions of people, all with the acquiescence and support of intellectuals who believed themselves to be progressive. This long and historic encounter saw many of our most gifted writers, artists, scientists, and intellectuals energetically engaged in opposing our own political and social institutions that comprised the foundations of the American character. The adversaries of freedom and democracy and individualism; namely, the communist movement, were never questioned by the progressives and intellectuals. They were complicit in socialist crimes, but they refused to confront their complicity in these crimes and give up the illusion that had made them inevitable.

They could have made one of two choices, either admit to the failures of their deeply held beliefs and recognize socialism and the communist movement as the failure that caused this destruction and abandon the Left. Following the communist collapse the great majority of the secular progressive intellectuals continued their war against the democracies of the West and are now professors teaching in some of the finest universities and colleges in the Western Hemisphere. They continue their destructive attacks on capitalism believing that the collapse of communism was the fault of those who attempted its reform. Many or most of them never seem to confront the moral issue posed by their destructive agendas. "The explicit agenda of critical theory is to undermine the credibility and authority of the status quo in order to prepare its annihilation." Critical theory is the coy self-description of the ideological Left. It defines itself by the totality of its rejection of the existing social order.

The words of one of the early leaders and founders of this nation serve as a haunting reminder of the need to protect and cherish our Christian heritage and our strength and innocence of character.

"A general dissolution of principles and manners will more surely overthrow the liberties of America than the whole force of the common enemy. While the people are virtuous, they cannot be subdued; but when once they lose their virtue then will be ready to surrender their liberties to the first external or internal invader" (Samuel Adams).

Our national character did not just happen; it developed over time from the beginning of those who braved a long and treacherous ocean voyage seeking religious freedom and culminated with the second inaugural address of Abraham Lincoln in which he stated, "The judgements of the Lord are true and righteous altogether." He ends the address with "With malice toward none; with charity for all; with firmness in the right, as God gives us to see the right, let us strive on to finish the work we are in; to bind the nation's wounds; to care for him who shall have borne the battle, and for his widow, and his orphan—to do all which may achieve and cherish a just and lasting peace, among ourselves, and with all nations." The Puritans brought with them the "dream of religious freedom" and the unique American ideal of *liberty, equality, and democracy*, defined in the Declaration of Independence as *life, liberty and the pursuit of happiness*, are unalienable rights endowed by their Creator. It is the very heart and soul of what America was to become. It was the emergence of the *national character, our American character*.

The American character is not a question of hope. The American character is the practical affirmation of God and the determination to live in the reality of His existence with the explanations in His Word. Without the Bible and without His Word there is no intellectually honest basis for what is man, what gives meaning, or what are absolute morals. Without this Holy Writ, God and man's understanding of Him, the human being will always look for substitutes: idols as visible gods, ideologies as master plans for life, personal meaning for the moment, and relative morals for personal desires.

It is the American character that dedicates in the preamble to the constitution that "We the people of the United States, in order to form a more perfect union," was signed in Convention Monday, September 17, 1787. The belief of the Founding Fathers in the perfection of God's creation is the strength of the American character and the grand expression of that character.

Hope is what those *loyalists* to the British crown had as they left this country during the revolution and fight for independence. They had hope that they would return one day when British rule was restored. Some went to Canada and others went back to the Old

Country. Most never returned once the hope had died and given way to a new nation. Those who went to Canada were more comfortable with the Old World and its mores.

Much has been spoken and written about *American courage* over the centuries. It is part of an indomitable spirit that has given this nation the ability to endure when faced with challenges that test our courage and our fears. Courage is the ability to act in the face of one's fears.

It was Theodore Roosevelt who listed and enumerated the hallmarks of the American character. They were "courage, vitality, perseverance, clean living, sturdy good sense, and an inflexible rectitude of soul." He loosely defined these traits as "character." Character determines the worth of the individual, and "what is true of the individual is true of the nation." Individualism, not individuality, is the vital word in describing the American character. It captures the essence, the enduring quality of all Americans. The desire for liberty and freedom of the American Revolution demonstrated that individual courage is not just the absence of fear; it is the ability to act and to face one's fears. Roosevelt was true to his progressive nature in believing that the state was the most important aspect of individuality which was to supplant the individualism taught by Christianity. It is necessary to explain the difference between individualism and individuality. Individualism is an ethical position, based on a rational understanding of human nature and the virtues which follow from it. By contrast, individuality is basically an aesthetic idea, sparks of color issuing from the gray mass of the collective. By holding parts of itself up for its own approval and acceptance, the socialist collective gathers what is needed to gain that approval and acceptance.

There were four public qualities, four key categories of civic virtues, the founders thought especially important for Americans, as a self-governing people, to acquire and practice. First, in order to be free, citizens of this new republic had to possess the virtue of self-reliance. The thought of formal welfare programs organized at the remote national level was unimaginable. Both God and country demanded unselfishness and charity and disregard for one's fellowman was inconsistent with "the Laws of Nature and of Nature's God."

What was not tolerable was laziness, refusal to work, or permanently living off of others. The notion of a "right to welfare" was the very type of dependency that undermined self-government.

Second, the founders valued those qualities that made for an assertive and spirited citizenry, possessing what Madison in *Federalist 57* described as that "vigilant and manly spirit which actuates the people of America, a spirit which nourishes freedom, and in return is nourished by it." Strong character included the virtues of courage, risk taking, and competitiveness. Courage is required so that citizens are willing to fight for the freedom and independence of their community and their country when necessary.

Third, the founders knew that a free people must possess and maintain a keen knowledge of the rights and responsibilities of citizenship. Americans must know about the nature of free government and the requirements of liberty. A good example of this type of knowledge is found in George Washington's first annual message to Congress.

> Knowledge is in every country the surest basis of public happiness. In one in which the measures of Government receive their impression so immediately from the sense of the Community as in ours it is proportionably essential. To the security of a free Constitution it contributes in various ways: By convincing those who are entrusted with the public administration, that every valuable end of Government is best answered by the enlightened confidence of the people: and by teaching the people themselves to know and to value their own rights; to discern and provide against invasions of them; to distinguish between oppression and the necessary exercise of lawful authority; between burthens proceeding from a disregard to their convenience and those resulting from the inevitable exigencies of Society; to discriminate the spirit of Liberty

> from that of licentiousness—cherishing the first,
> avoiding the last, and uniting a speedy, but tem-
> perate vigilance against encroachments, with an
> inviolable respect to the Laws.

Knowledge of the first principles of liberty is essential and must be a cultivated virtue for free government.

A fourth virtue is implied in Washington's call for the people "to discriminate the spirit of Liberty from that of licentiousness," a self-governing people must possess great self-restraint and a strong sense of personal and public moderation. In general, the founders drew on the chief virtues inculcated by the long Western tradition of faith and reason: prudence, justice, moderation, courage, hope, and charity. The American founders sought to establish the consti-tutional basis for a society that could inspire these moral qualities in the American character, strengthened by the religious faith held by nearly all Americans. They also understood that the practice of these virtues was the essence of self-government in the individual and the firmest foundation for an independent, self-governed society. To instill these virtues, they looked to the character-forming role of law, education, and the institutions of civil society, especially religious institutions and the family.

The importance of the Holy Bible is clearly a vital organ of the American character. America is not now nor has it ever been a secular nation. Its government is secular as expressed in the first amendment to the constitution, but as a nation America has, since its conception, been a powerful religious idea. And the American character is indeed a religion in its own right.

The vision of the *American character* began with the Puritans coming and culminated with the second inaugural address of Abraham Lincoln: "With malice toward none; with charity for all; with firmness in the right, as God gives us to see the right..." America is a biblical republic; it is not a secular republic. It was always and will always be in accordance with the vision of the Founding Fathers.

In the history of ideas it is well known that bad ideas can have lethal consequences. At the heart of the darkness inside the great mid-twentieth century tyrannies were these expressions of atheistic humanism, communism, fascism, Nazism. Henri de Lubac discerned the lethal effects of the marriage between modern technology and the culture-shaping ideas borne by atheistic humanism. "It is not true, as is sometimes said, that man cannot organize the world without God. What is true is that without God, he can only organize it against man."

As stated earlier all of these tyrannies were expressions of atheistic humanism, and they received their impetus from the *positivism* of Auguste Comte (empirical science is humanity's only reliable tutor), subjectivism, and the materialism of Marx. The main tenet of these philosophies is that only phenomena are knowable as received by the external senses. This leaves no room for such phenomena as moral experiences or introspection.

In his book *The American Commonwealth*, James Bryce defined the American character. Bryce wrote that America's constitution "forms the mind and temper of the people." He continues with "It makes them feel that to comprehend their supreme instrument of government is a personal duty, incumbent on each one of them. It familiarizes them with, it attaches them by ties of pride and reverence to, those fundamental truths on which the constitution is based." Our national character is biblical-based, and we are a biblical republic. Our Founding Fathers were strongly influenced by the Holy Bible, and they used the Bible as a guide in forming our republican form of government.

What the Declaration of Independence did was define the principles of the American Republic: that all men are created equal and hence have equal natural rights as a gift of the Creator.

Our Founding Fathers knew from the beginning that if democracy were to inevitably survive, men and women of strong character and faith would be needed as leaders of this nation *under God* and that it did not stop with them, but that it required men and women of strong moral character in all aspects of American life.

Since the end of World War I, our institutions and our national character have come under ever-increasing attack from those who then claim protection under the first amendment of the constitution.

I do not wish to deny them this right nor to deny the principle of free speech. I do wish, however, to stop the erosion of the rights of the many by the working agenda of the few.

James Madison recognized a faction as a group adverse to the rights of other citizens and states that "there are two methods of curing the mischiefs of faction: the one, by removing its cause; the other by controlling its effects."

To remove the causes of faction would require the destruction of liberty, for "liberty is to faction what air is to fire, an ailment without which it instantly expires."

He sees the latent causes of faction as sown in the nature of man, which leads to the conclusion that relief is to be sought only in the means of controlling its effects, and this relief is supplied by the republican principle of elected representatives who then pass laws by which this republic is governed.

However, that is not the end of the argument, in the *Federalist Papers* essay number 10, Madison comes to deal with the crucial problem of breaking or controlling the violence of faction, whether amounting to a majority or minority, by offering the crucial assumption that a broader republic with its national congress representing many sections and groups would overcome and control the violence of faction, be it either majority or minority.

Madison saw government as a necessary evil that must be curbed, not an instrument for the realization of men's higher ideals or the broader interests of the nation. The historian Richard Hofstadter has called this a harmonious system of mutual frustration.

The first amendment states that "Congress shall make no law respecting an establishment of religion, or prohibiting the free exercise thereof; or abridging the freedom of speech, or of the press; or the right of the people peaceably to assemble, and to petition the Government for a redress of grievances."

For too long now we have seen the courts uphold the rights of a lone dissenter only to take away the rights of the many. The ACLU and the judiciary prefer to interpret Christianity as an establishment of religion rather than faith in a higher being that the founders of this nation trusted for guidance while defining this nation, its Christian heritage and its constitution, only to ignore the next sentence in the Bill of Rights which states that congress shall make no law prohibiting the free exercise thereof. Perhaps we should change the wording of the constitution to say that congress and federal judges shall make no law prohibiting the free exercise thereof.

In this instance it would appear that Madison's thinking and his central aim to stop people from turning easily to the government for help is a lost exercise of the intellect. The judiciary branch of government, the federal judges who are not elected but appointed and therefore are not representatives of the people as such, have given to themselves a power that the constitution does not give even to congress.

The real issue then is whether or not any federal judge has the right to interfere with state actions that may or may not have anything to do with or constitute an establishment of religion.

The tenth amendment to the constitution states that "The powers not delegated to the United States by the constitution, nor prohibited by it to the States, are reserved to the States respectively, or to the people." The power to make laws regarding an establishment of religion, having been explicitly withheld from the United States by the tenth amendment, is therefore reserved to the states or to the people.

The attack on the constitution probably started with the administration of Theodore Roosevelt. Roosevelt combined the strong national government of Hamilton with the democratic faith of Jefferson. Roosevelt would use Hamiltonian means to achieve Jeffersonian ends. The progressive movement was the child of Woodrow Wilson and Edward M. House, who began forming the administrative state, placing the running of the country in the hands of unelected officials running the lives of American citizens. Wilson and House began their assault with the Federal Reserve Act and the sixteenth amendment that established the Internal Revenue Service as an administrative organ to assist Congress with their power and ability to lay and collect taxes on income. Power was being taken away from the people and placed in the hands of administrators much like the ones in the book written by Edward M. House, *Phillip Dru:*

Administrator, with a subtitle *A Story of Tomorrow*. It could actually be "A Story of Today." With the election of Barack Obama and his ideology of income redistribution, the progressives have their hero.

The Warren Court and their propensity use social doctrine and social theory to make decisions rather than through cases of law. Roe v. Wade, though decided in 1973, certainly was a critical juncture that opened up for Justice Harry Blackmun and his view that the document he had sworn to uphold could and should be altered according to liberal prejudice and judicial whim rather than the republic's rule by law and the founders' idea of principles that do not change.

In the realm of the criminal justice system, the Warren Court, with the liberal majority of Warren, Douglas, Black, Brennan, Clark, and Stewart totally rewrote, with profound social consequences, major constitutional doctrines governing race relations, the administration of criminal justice, and the operation of the political process.

Now we see the institution of marriage coming under attack from the ACLU, the NEA or National Education Association Teachers Union, the judiciary, and a minority group with an agenda claiming that they wish only to have the same rights as married couples of both sexes. This is far from the truth, and their attempts to equate their quest with that of the Civil Rights Movement is nothing but an attempt to impose an acceptance of a lifestyle that is alien to Christians and all who believe that heterosexuality is the norm. Judicial tyranny must not and cannot be tolerated in Massachusetts or anywhere else in this country.

As long as they continue to legislate from the bench, we, as citizens, must resist. The political agenda of the homosexual community can be seen only as one more example of an attack upon our economic and social conditions, our institutions, and our national character. Forgive me, but it is time. It is time to take a stand. It is time to reclaim our rights as Christians and proclaim the principles of the constitution and the Declaration of Independence with enough vigor that those who seek to attack our national character begin to tremble. We are now, now and forever, "one nation under God."

Let us always remember to set forth asking His blessing and His help. We must remain that "shining city upon a hill" that John

Winthrop wrote about while aboard the *Arabella* in 1630 bound for Massachusetts. For as the Psalm was written long ago, "Except the Lord build the house, they labour in vain that build it: except the Lord keep the city, the watchman awakens but in vain."

A notable quote by Herbert Croly says, "For better or worse, democracy cannot be disentangled from an aspiration toward human perfectibility, and hence from the adoption of measures looking in the direction of realizing such an aspiration."

Believe in the perfectibility of all mankind. It is a never-ending struggle of the progressive mind and one that is truly revolutionary, but America is able to recognize her failures and continues to believe and to strive for liberty and not equality. All men are created equal by their Creator not by the state, but through freedom and liberty they are given equal opportunity to achieve their level according to their talents.

CHAPTER 3

— ❧ —

The Constitution in Crisis

Since the end of World War II the Supreme Court has actively engaged in rewriting the liberties enumerated in the constitution. The Declaration of Independence, as well as the *Federalist Papers*, document the Founding Fathers' plan for limited government originally set forth in the constitution and Bill of Rights. It demonstrates that the Founding Fathers were all men of strong and, needless to say, Christian faith and that we are now and forever "one nation under God."

The aim of the body politic, in their struggle to govern, must be a continuing effort to make those in power more responsive and responsible to the democratic wishes of the people of this great republic. Instead we have seen the executive and legislative branches of government willing to relinquish and abandon the system of checks and balances afforded them to a judicial branch who wish to govern by fiat from the bench. These are unelected officials, and since they are not elected but appointed and therefore are not representatives of the people as such, they have given to themselves a power that the constitution gives only to Congress as the legislative branch and to the states. The judicial branch and the Supreme Court, in particular, seek to establish their existence as a power elite who, by distant vision and their capacity to see things whole, come to play a superior role.

Thomas Jefferson once said that "The judiciary of the United States is the subtle corps of sappers and miners constantly working under ground to undermine the foundations of our confederated fabric. They are construing our constitution from a coordination of a general and special government to a general and supreme one alone."

As this "one nation under God" finds itself becoming enslaved by those in the federal judiciary and the Supreme Court who make such laws from the bench and then seek to enforce them, the question then becomes, is the public bound to yield obedience to laws to which they cannot give their approbation? Shameless judicial activism is forcing Christians to take a stand. It is a stand that is long overdue.

Those who claim to have a "live-and-let-live" philosophy are either fooling themselves or are fooled by the radical Left and the media hype spewed almost daily by the liberal press. How do you remain tolerant when those whom you are allowing to live thusly are busily building organizations that have political agendas that are by design aimed at denying you your right to *live* as you would *let them live*? There can no longer be a body of people who refuse to take a stand in the face of moral decay. Those who would allow secular corruption of our children by not allowing prayer in school, by not allowing the Ten Commandments to be displayed, by proclaiming that any display of the birth of Christ in the form of a manger scene on the courthouse lawn or public school grounds or any public property is an establishment of religion are not only wrong but dangerous and deliberate. We can no longer be tolerant of judges and politicians who wish to destroy our constitution and our reliance on old identities. They must be revitalized and reaffirmed, not blurred and compromised. We, as Christians, in order to survive, need to rediscover theological firmness and doctrinal clarity.

Alexander Hamilton, in the *Federalist Papers* No. 81, wrote, "[T]here is not a syllable in the plan under consideration which directly empowers the national courts to construe the laws according to the spirit of the Constitution."

Previously, Hamilton had written in the *Federalist Papers* No. 78, "[T]hough individual oppression may now and then proceed from the courts of justice, the general liberty of the people can never be endangered from that quarter."

The virtue of intolerance, by now, should outweigh our blindness to the facts. We, as a republican nation, ruled by law given to us by elected representatives and guided by principles that do not change, are not bound by laws coming from supremacist judges who have exceeded their constitutional authority. In this democratic nation all power is ultimately vested in *the people*. Such knowledge does not help much in defining how power is exercised. Who holds the power and who has the ability to act and carry out the functions of government is the key to the separation of powers. We can no longer afford to be tolerant.

We have seen the Supreme Court justices, since FDR populated the court with judicial activists who believe that the constitution is a living document subject to all manner of judicial interpretation and who legislate from the bench by issuing rulings based on their personal interpretation of the constitution or that of the liberal Left.

Prior to the ascent of Franklin D. Roosevelt to the presidency, the courts were still populated with originalists, who properly rendered legal interpretation based on strict construction of the constitution's *original intent*. It is true that Woodrow Wilson pioneered the doctrine of the "Living constitution" but it was the Roosevelt administration's goal to transform American politics by creating vast client constituencies who depended on the government for their livelihood. This was first and foremost a philosophical vision not an economic one. The difference between *original intent* and *limited constitution* of the Founding Fathers and the *living constitution* which is the ideal of progressives and liberals was more plainly expressed by Woodrow Wilson when he insisted that "living political constitutions must be *Darwinian* in structure and practice." The Declaration of Independence affirms that human rights are fixed and unchanging. They are endowed by our Creator and as such are fixed and unchanging, but with a living constitution human rights become historical or evolutionary and are dependent upon government to grant or take away as they see fit to do.

In a speech to the nation on March 9, 1937, however, President Roosevelt explained to the American people that his intent was to stop the judiciary from becoming policymakers and not stray from their constitutional role as the highest judicial court of the land. This was in reaction to the court's conservative make-up of justices appointed in the 1920s. President Roosevelt had sent legislation to Congress to increase the court by as many as six members in an attempt to pack the court with liberal judges who would not block his New Deal legislative agenda. It was the first attempt to politicize the Supreme Court. The president lost the legislative battle but won the war.

Justice Scalia states that "activism becomes problematic when the Court strikes down laws for reasons that have no grounding in the constitution—as the Court did to FDR's New Deal programs in the 1930s, angering the Left, and then again when it invalidated state laws restricting abortion in the 1970s, provoking the Right." Scalia believes that words and laws say what they mean and mean exactly what they say, and as the supreme law in the constitution of the United States, judges should rely on the text as it is written. Scalia defines himself as a "textualist."

The institutions examined here all seem to have the same failing. They are inclined to see government and the art of governing as requiring the existence of a power elite. The late Senator Kennedy and others of the democratic Left who feel that the judicial branch of government is the only branch sensitive to social justice agendas are inclined to see themselves as the only ones with distant vision and capacity to see things whole and that they must come to play a superior role. It is socialism (atheistic humanism) in disguise. It has disguised itself as progressivism, liberalism, secular humanism, and eventually environmentalism, feminism, and a vast assortment of other social justice causes.

Christianity teaches individualism as seen in the radical command of Jesus Christ to love your neighbor as yourself and, as such, can only be sustained through knowledge and faith. We, the people, cannot ignore reality for long and dismiss the interests of the nation as a whole as alien to our own interests. We are one nation and one people, and we must live, work, govern, and be governed in the same manner. Only through knowledge, high purpose, and the use of self-restraint in the exercise of power can this nation determine whether a government of separated powers will continue to endure.

Surely our governors, state legislators, and the United States Congress and senators can see that they have the power, as our elected representatives, to change the direction and destruction of our constitution or face the consequence of the people changing them.

We hear them, the conservative media talk show hosts, day in and day out talking about the ACLU and the liberal Left, the disinformation of the mainstream media, and they keep us informed of the real issues that we face. We can easily find agreement with them, but we must act in order to change the current direction. Our nation is experiencing a power struggle.

Secular or atheistic humanism and moral relativism are attempting to gain power through the reversal of human norms, natural law, and the social institutions that are so necessary for the continuance of mankind. These are the principles that guide the progressive and/or liberal politics and politicians.

In his book *The Everlasting Man*, G. K. Chesterton described this reversal process as the "theology of demons" and said that it was sadistically antihuman and anti-childhood. It is intrinsically evil. It is a malignancy-filled system of philosophy posturing as something seemingly innocuous in order to infect Christendom and Christianity in the United States.

With the growing strength of secular humanism and their agenda to instill a dualistic thought process of nature/grace or the divide between fact/value along with the rise of Darwinism and his naturalistic mechanism for the origin of life comes the notion that reason is religiously neutral. Secularism and naturalism are falsely promoted as being neutral while biblical views are dismissed as biased private opinions. The desired effect of secular or atheistic humanism is that Christians will abandon the world of ideas and the Christian worldview to the secularists.

It was the Roosevelt administration's goal to transform American politics by creating vast client constituencies who depended on the government for their livelihood. This was first and foremost a philosophical vision not an economic one. The difference between *original intent* and *limited constitution* of the Founding Fathers and the *living constitution* which is the ideal of progressives and liberals was more plainly expressed by Woodrow Wilson when he insisted that "living political constitutions must be Darwinian in structure and practice." The Declaration of Independence affirms that human rights are fixed and unchanging. They are endowed by our Creator and as such are fixed and unchanging, but with a living constitution human rights become historical or evolutionary and are dependent upon government to grant or take away as they see fit to do.

In reading Justice Joseph Story's *Commentaries on the Constitution of the United States*, you will find that the first amendment was enacted for a very narrow purpose and to prohibit a very specific offense.

The founders not only chose not to establish federally any particular denomination of Christianity, they further never intended the first amendment to become a vehicle to promote a pluralism of other religions. As Justice Story explained in his commentaries, "The real object of the First Amendment was not to countenance, much less to advance, Mahometanism, or Judaism, or infidelity, by prostrating Christianity; but to exclude all rivalry among Christian sects."

In reality, Islam must be excluded from any first amendment consideration because in Islam there is no separation of church and state, as the liberals try to claim in our constitution. In Islam they are one and the same; there is no separation. Islamic groups openly claim that their goal is not to peaceably assimilate into Western society on equal footing with other religious persons and groups or other religions; they want to dominate completely in all aspects of the culture.

With the growing strength of secular humanism and its agenda to instill a dualistic thought process of nature/grace or the divide between fact/value, along with the rise of Darwinism and his naturalistic mechanism for the origin of life, comes the notion that reason is religiously neutral. Secularism and naturalism are falsely promoted as being neutral while biblical views are dismissed as biased private opinions. The desired effect of secular or atheistic humanism is that Christians will abandon the world of ideas and the Christian worldview to the secularists.

It was the Roosevelt administration's goal to transform American politics by creating vast client constituencies who depended on the

government for their livelihood. This was first and foremost a philosophical vision, not an economic one. The difference between *original intent* and *limited constitution* of the Founding Fathers and the *living Constitution,* which is the ideal of progressives and liberals, was more plainly expressed by Woodrow Wilson when he insisted that "living political constitutions must be Darwinian in structure and practice." The Declaration of Independence affirms that human rights are fixed and unchanging. They are endowed by our Creator and as such are fixed and unchanging, but with a living constitution human rights become historical or evolutionary and are dependent upon government to grant or take away as they see fit to do.

In reading Justice Joseph Story's *Commentaries on the Constitution of the United States,* you will find that the first amendment was enacted for a very narrow purpose and to prohibit a very specific offense.

The founders not only chose not to establish federally any particular denomination of Christianity; they further never intended the first amendment to become a vehicle to promote a pluralism of other religions. As Justice Story explained in his commentaries, "The real object of the First Amendment was not to countenance, much less to advance, Mahometanism, or Judaism, or infidelity, by prostrating Christianity; but to exclude all rivalry among Christian sects."

In reality, Islam must be excluded from any first amendment consideration because in Islam there is no separation of church and state. They are one and the same; there is no separation. Islamic groups openly claim that their goal is not to peaceably assimilate into Western society on equal footing with other religious persons and groups or other religions; they want to dominate completely in all aspects of the culture.

The words of one of the early leaders and founders of this nation serve as a haunting reminder of the need to protect and cherish our Christian heritage and our strength and innocence of character.

"A general dissolution of principles and manners will more surely overthrow the liberties of America than the whole force of the common enemy. While the people are virtuous, they cannot be subdued; but when once they lose their virtue then will be ready to surrender their liberties to the first external or internal invader," said Samuel Adams.

We are at war with Islam and with Shari'ah Law, that is undeniable. Why do academics who teach at the conservative institutions of higher learning continue to destroy the idea of America's Founding Fathers being of strong faith and Christian belief? Michael Babcock PhD, in his book *Unchristian America: Living With Faith in a Nation That Was Never Under God,* claims that America has been a four-hundred-year laboratory experiment in living out the humanistic values of the modern age. He discounts the fact that the Founding Fathers invoked God's name in nearly everything they wrote, as described by Dr. Warren Throckmorton of Grove City College.

President Bush and his advisers, one of which was Professor David Forte, held the conviction that Islamic terrorists and Muslim aggressors are, by definition, heretics and not *real* Muslims. Bush and Forte were also proponents of Ecumenical Jihad and shared two fallacies. One is the faulty understanding of Islamic theology which leads them to imagine that *Allah* is more or less interchangeable with the *god* of other monotheists. But as Francis Schaeffer explains, "The Bible is clear: there is a moral law of the universe. And that basic law is the character of God Himself. He is not a contentless God, but a God with a character. His character is the law of the universe. When He reveals this character to us in verbalized, propositional form, we have the commands of God for men. Thus there are absolutes and categories; the law which the God who exists has revealed and which is based upon His character is final. This is the biblical position. The Bible's teaching alone gives moral answers to men."

According to Alexander Solzhenitsyn, "The line separating good and evil passes not through states, nor between classes, nor between political parties either but right through every human heart—and through all human hearts."

CHAPTER 4

———— ∽ ————

The Crescent and the Cross

Islam Is an Ideology and a False Religion
Saving Our Judeo-Christian Identity

Finally, my brethren, be strong in the Lord, and in the
power of his might. Put on the whole armour of God, that
ye may be able to stand against the wiles of the devil.
—Ephesians 6:10–11

It is very disturbing to listen to Western leaders, diplomats, and others who are responsible for setting and establishing policy toward Islam and terrorism when they refuse to face the reality of Muslim aggression that has all through history been and continues to be "Jihad without end." The Muslim does not hate us because they hate freedom; they hate us because we are not Muslim. Islam has been at war with us, as Christians, for fourteen centuries. Why do we not see that it is not simply radical Islam who is trying to kill us? According to Islam, the two people who killed fourteen people in San Bernardino, California, are, in the eyes of the prophet, good Muslims because they followed the dictates of their holy book, the Koran, in killing infidels. The only bad Muslims are those who reject the teachings of the prophet and come to know Jesus Christ as Lord and Savior. We are at war with Islam; make no mistake about this. We are at war with Islam, and there is no room for coexistence. Islam and its interpretation of the Koran must be destroyed as an evil entity. Once we lose our Judeo Christian identity that this country was founded upon and the Declaration of Independence and the constitution that was written and instilled with natural law and Judeo Christian values, this country is doomed, and that is what Islam is counting on.

It is not difficult to understand the actions and inactions of President Barack Obama regarding Islam and Muslims. He points to the fact that recent mass shootings in San Bernardino and Orlando have been carried out by United States citizens. Obama blamed the attacks on the proliferation of guns in the United States, and he wanted to disarm the American people. His insane argument that an armed person in those gun-free zones would have caused more fatalities is the total lack of logic. The common denominator in all of this is that they are all Muslims. Whether they had ties to ISIS or other Jihadist groups is not important. They were following the dictates of Islam. We are at war with Islam and have been for the last fourteen centuries. It is time to face the facts. Obama is aiding the Islamic triumph and implementation of Sharia Law. He has gone out of his way to destroy the constitution. His entire game plan is to protect and promote the world of Islam and Muslims in this country.

According to Islam, the Koran is to be recited and not subjected to analytical study by a reasoning mind: "Whoever so interprets the Quran according to his opinion, let him seek his abode in the fire." In the words of Muhammad, "Dispute about the Quran is infidelity." Muslims do not wish to assimilate in America; they want to dominate and control. They are laughing at us. They wish to establish Islam as the one true religion and Allah as the only god. Muslim propaganda, through organizations such as CAIR, has told us that they are a "religion of peace" and that they worship the same god, but there is only one God, the Triune God of Christianity. His Truth is Truth with a capital *T*.

"Of all the major religions known to man, the teaching of Islam makes it the least amenable to dialogue with other faiths." There is a reason for this, and it is the fact that Islam is an invented religion. C. S. Lewis expressed it thusly, "If Christianity was something we were making up, of course we could make it easier. But it is not. We cannot compete, in simplicity, with people who are inventing religions. How could we? We are dealing with fact. Of course anyone can be simple if he has no facts to bother about."

It is time that the world recognizes the truth about Islam. It is not a *religion* of peace, and their diagram for world conquest is documented in their holy book, the Koran. It is an ideology that uses religion to further its ambition for world dominance and the imposition of Shariah (Islamic Law). There is no justice in the world without Shariah Law, according to Islam. They hide behind their religion and, while using the benefits and freedoms of a republican democracy, claim religious intolerance and persecution when critical articles are written about the "prophet" or the "religion" of peace.

The house of Islam, long before today's political correctness, has never been known as a religion of peace, and the sooner we, in the West, recognize that this is an ideology which uses religion for war and aggression and that throughout the world Christians and Jews are being persecuted and murdered by Muslims, we will remain in grave danger. It is called fascism—Islamo-Fascism.

Our past secretary of state, Condoleezza Rice, must have been living in a different world if she considered the Gaza pullout to be *successful and effective.* In the past, Israel has been eager and even willing to go far beyond the multiple and unreciprocated concessions it has already made. The United States continues to pressure Israel into making the same mistakes of the past, which will only produce the same outcome. Will we never learn that Palestinian promises are meant to be broken?

Why do we continue to attempt to deal with the Muslim world and the world of Islam when we know that they view diplomacy as a sign of weakness? Obviously we have forgotten the lessons of history when Churchill stood almost alone against Nazi aggression and the British and French pusillanimous policy of appeasement. This is a serious chess game, and we must not forget the roles of power, strength, and strategy.

Islam was spread by the sword from its beginning. We have experienced fourteen centuries of Islamic conquest by the sword.

Mohammed conquered the Arabian Peninsula in twenty years, and within one hundred years, most of Spain was conquered. It took Charles Martel in 732 stopping them at Tours in the West, then they were stopped in the East at the gates of Vienna in 1450. This history shows the aggressive nature of a Muslim "religion" that wants the West to believe that they are "a religion of peace."

Now we see one more example of Muslim and Islamic aggression with widespread rioting in France. Fox News had a Catholic priest on a news show during the time of the riots. The priest, while well-intentioned but very naïve, was in France trying to explain to the world after having interviews with Muslim school teens that the riots have nothing to do with religion. Everything the Muslim does is about *religion* as it is used to show their hatred of Christians and Jews. That religion is Islam, and the sooner we face the truth, the better. Do we not understand this fact that Islam is intent upon carrying out their worldwide "Jihad without end?"

There is a long history of Nazi Germany and Adolf Hitler and the influence of Hitler on Arab nationalism and Muslim fanaticism. Islam and Fascist ideology have shared the same goal since long before the First World War. They share a hatred of Zionism and a desire to destroy all of Israel. Islam's hatred of Jews and Christians was codified, according to Serge Trifkovic in his book *The Sword of the Prophet* on the eve of the first crusade.

The Nazi connection to radical Islamic terrorism is well documented and began in 1935 with the shah of Iran, the father of the man who was deposed in 1979. He was a Nazi sympathizer. He hated the Jews. The name of the country was changed from Persia to Iran, which literally means "land of the Aryans." Later, the same shah welcomed Haj Mohammad Amin al-Husseini, the exiled grand mufti of Jerusalem, into the country. The mufti was on the run because of his pro-Nazi work and his efforts in attempting to bring the Jewish holocaust to the Middle East.

Muslim aggression has all through history been and continues to be "Jihad without end." The Muslim does not hate us because they hate freedom; they hate us because we are not Muslim. It is a religious crusade to create a Muslim world dominated by Islam. This

is not new; it was going on long before Pope Urban II declared in 1095 at Clermont that "A race absolutely alien to God has invaded the land of Christians, has reduced the people with sword, rapine and flame."

The house of Islam is in a permanent state of war with the lands that surround it. Of course it can be interrupted by temporary truces, but peace will only come with the completion of global conquest.

In his foreword to *T. E. Lawrence in War and Peace*, Professor Michael Clarke, director of the International Policy Institute, King's College, London, wrote in June 2005 that Lawrence came to understand the principles of effective counter-insurgency. He learned from brutal experience that insurgencies worked not by confronting the enemy at its center, but by stretching it out like elastic. Insurgencies by themselves would seldom defeat an enemy, but they could deny victory almost indefinitely, while more conventional forces, be they military or political, would work to defeat it.

The *war on terror* is what we have chosen to call this challenge to our freedom, but we continue to sleepwalk while our culture is being systematically destroyed from within. Since the crusades, Islam has tried to portray itself as a victim of religious persecution when in reality it was an excuse for fourteen centuries of conquest.

There has been no hijacking of a beautiful religion as President Bush kept trying to tell the American people. Look around you and you will see in every part of the world Christians being killed by Islam in the name of Allah. The house of Islam is in a state of permanent war, and the choice of conversion or death is the only option offered to Christians and Jews. It is an ideology, not a religion. It is a race and an ideology totally alien to God that has invaded the land of Christians, and we must defeat this radical Islamist ideology just as we defeated the Soviet communist ideology and Nazism and Adolf Hitler's brand of anti-Semitism.

There is no substitute for victory. Unconditional surrender is the only attitude allowed if we are to defeat *terrorism*. We cannot wait for Islam to be reformed or to win the hearts and minds of the mullahs. They view diplomacy and negotiation as a sign of weakness.

Jerusalem is sacred to the Muslim belief as the city from which the prophet Muhammad ascended into heaven, but if the God of Christianity is correct in His teachings through Jesus Christ as all Christians throughout the world believe, then Muhammad, along with Abu Musab al-Zarqawi and the nineteen Muslims who flew airplanes into the World Trade Center, the Pentagon, and a field in Pennsylvania, are in hell where they belong. They are despicable, thieves, liars, dirty, awful without a redeeming feature, not martyrs. Their mind-set on "Jihad without end" leaves no room for negotiation or diplomacy. Perhaps we, as Christians, should offer Muslims the same alternative they offer to the Christian world: convert or die. I fully understand that this notion defies true Christian belief, but if Christianity is to survive, then the issue of self-defense is an undeniable fact of life.

C. S. Lewis, in *Mere Christianity*, answered the question of the cluttered complexity of Christianity. He explained that "if Christianity was something we were making up, of course we could make it easier. But it is not. We cannot compete, in simplicity, with people who are inventing religions. How could we? We are dealing with Fact. Of course anyone can be simple if he has no facts to bother about."

President Bush and his advisers, one of which was Professor David Forte, held the conviction that Islamic terrorists and Muslim aggressors are, by definition, heretics and not *real* Muslims. Bush and Forte were also proponents of Ecumenical Jihad and shared two fallacies. One is the faulty understanding of Islamic theology which leads them to imagine that *Allah* is more or less interchangeable with the *god* of other monotheists. But as Francis Schaeffer explains, "The Bible is clear: there is a moral law of the universe. And that basic law is the character of God Himself. He is not a contentless God, but a God with a character. His character is the law of the universe. When He reveals this character to us in verbalized, propositional form, we have the commands of God for men. Thus there are absolutes and categories; the law which the God who exists has revealed and which is based upon His character is final. This is the biblical position. The Bible's teaching alone gives moral answers to men."

Secondly, Christians, in order to survive, need to rediscover theological firmness and doctrinal and moral clarity. Resistance to secularism will come from old identities revitalized and reaffirmed, not distorted and compromised. In fighting Islam-Fascism, a new objective is needed—one that shows that Jesus Christ is Lord and that Allah is a false god. There is only one true God—the God of total truth.

I do not wish to pursue the alternative of convert or die to the Muslim. I do not wish to burn the Qur'an. I would rather pray that Muslims come to Christianity as they burn the Qur'an and grasp the Holy Bible as the Word of God and the total truth of Jesus Christ. We should not burn the so-called holy book of Islam. It must be shown to be nothing more than a faithful mirror of the life and character of its author, the Prophet Muhammad, who, through the gradual decline of his character, became a "conscious impostor and open sensualist."

No one wants to admit that we are engaged in a crusade for the survival of Christianity, but that is exactly what we, Christians, are facing today. It is not a holy war; it is a global war of conquest and Islamic expansion by the sword for the purpose of the imposition of Islamic law on a global basis. That is their goal for America, and Christianity is the only thing standing in their way.

The American character is the practical affirmation of God and the determination to live in the reality of His existence with the explanations in His Word. Without His Word there is no intellectually honest basis for what is man, what gives meaning, or what are absolute morals. Without this God and man's understanding of Him, the human being will always go for substitutes: idols as visible gods, ideologies as master plans for life, personal meaning for the moment, and relative morals for personal desires. The importance of the Holy Bible is clearly a vital organ of the American character. America is not now nor has it ever been a secular nation, nor has it ever been a theocracy. America has, since its conception, been a powerful religious idea, and the American character is indeed a religion in its own right, and that religion is Christianity.

Democrats and especially Hillary Clinton and President Obama are telling us that we are not at war with Islam. The truth of the matter is that Islam has been at war with the world for fourteen centuries. Somehow we fail to recognize this fact, yet if you look at the picture of Abaaoud, what is he holding in his right hand? It is a copy of the Kuran, which tells us that Allah "does not love the unbelievers." Allah's absolute sovereignty means that his *closeness* to man does not imply a two-way relationship; man's experience of Allah is impossible. Any attempt to verbalize such a notion would imply heretical encroachment on his absolute transcendence. Serge Trifkovic, in his book *The Sword of the Prophet*, has explained, "That transcendence is so absolute in its implication that Allah is Oneness in himself that we are led to conclude that Allah is the only being with real existence, and the rest of his creation has a contingent existence. Ultimately, it may be argued that Allah is All, which is the essence of pantheism." We simply do not need to bring any more Muslims to this country, and that is what Obama is attempting to do. We are in danger of being overrun. It is insanity not to oppose Islam and their egregious abuses of our constitution. We cannot afford to lose our Judeo Christian identity. If we do, this country is doomed.

According to Robert Jeffress, senior pastor of First Baptist Church, Dallas, "Government is never called upon to forgive. Government is never called upon to turn the other cheek. The responsibility of government, according to the word of God, is to protect its citizens."

Read more here: http://www.star-telegram.com/news/local/community/fort-worth/article45607614.html#storylink=cpy.

CHAPTER 5

―― ✑ ――

The War on Terror: Our Reason to Fight

Radical Islam is just what the doctor ordered. It is what multiculturalism has been waiting for all along. The beauty of multiculturalism is that you can choose which side of the war you want to fight on—either *for* or *against*, whichever one fits for the moment. The Barack Obamas and the Eric Holders of the world speak with disdain about the America that they live in and then proceed to take advantage of each and every aspect of our culture that makes them wealthier than they deserve. They are un-American and traitors, and yet our leaders in Congress refuse to brand them as such proclaiming this as a fine example of the virtues of the multicultural state. Our leaders congratulate themselves on the boundless tolerance that this republic affords even as the forces of the multicultural activists and ideologues consume this republic.

The liberal Left refuses to acknowledge that our unity arises from an ideology and value system that is more right of center than they are willing to admit. They wish to take away our unalienable rights and replace them with a fascist ideology very similar to communism. They like to call it secular humanism, but it is still fascism that denies the reality of a supreme being who grants us those unalienable human rights.

The *war on terror* is what we have chosen to call this challenge to our freedom; however, it is really a battle for survival. We are at war with Islam, and it is a question of survival in the sense that

35

Islam's goal is world domination and the imposition of Sharia Law, but we continue to sleepwalk while our culture is being systematically destroyed from within. Since the crusades, Islam has tried to portray themselves as victims of religious persecution when in reality it was an excuse for fourteen centuries of conquest and hatred. Islam is the complete embodiment of *evil*, and we in America have somehow forgotten that evil exists in this world. Hardly anyone preaches against evil any longer. The churches have forgotten that evil in the form of Satan or Hitler or Stalin or Mao Tse-tung ever existed. Islam is real and it is evil.

There has been no hijacking of a beautiful religion as President Bush kept trying to tell the American people. Look around you and you will see in every part of the world Christians being killed by Islam in the name of Allah. The house of Islam is in a state of permanent war, and the choice of conversion or death is the only option offered to Christians and Jews. While Islam is called a religion, it is also an ideology. It is an ideology totally alien to Christianity that has invaded the land of Christians, and we, as Christians, must defeat this radical Islamist ideology just as we defeated the Soviet communist ideology and Nazism and Adolf Hitler's brand of anti-Semitism. It is an ideology where the leaders, the Imams and Ayatollahs, of this false "religion" encourage their followers to seek martyrdom as a means of attaining heaven, while they themselves do not follow this route. This is a "religion," with a fanatical ideology seeking world domination. It is a cult of death that worships suicide and promotes and exalts death and desecration. They demand the freedom of speech and religion granted to Americans by our constitution, and yet they deny those freedoms in Muslim-controlled countries. It is one-way multiculturalism, and it is part of their plan. Islam seeks the advantage in each and every situation.

Muslim aggression has all through history been and continues to be "Jihad without end." The Muslim does not hate us because they hate freedom; they hate us because we are not Muslim. It is a "religious" crusade to create a Muslim world dominated by Islamic ideology. This is not new; it was going on long before Pope Urban II declared that "A race absolutely alien to God has invaded the land

of Christians, has reduced the people with sword, rapine and flame." The pope continued by stating, "On whom, therefore, does the task lie of avenging this, of redeeming this situation, if not on you, upon whom above all nations God has bestowed outstanding glory in arms, magnitude of heart, litheness of body and strength to humble anyone who resists you."

There is no substitute for victory. Unconditional surrender is the only attitude needed if we are to defeat *terrorism*. We cannot wait for Islam to be reformed or to win the hearts and minds of the mullahs. They view diplomacy and negotiation as a sign of weakness. Our country needs a new objective in fighting Islamo-Fascism—one that destroys their will to fight, not ours. In World War II we fought a war of *unconditional surrender* with both Germany and Japan. We brought about democratic reforms following their total defeat. We cannot hope to bring democracy to Iraq until that will to fight is taken from the terrorists through defeat and/or surrender.

Some have made the assertion that Islam was "born in the full light of history." That statement is incorrect since *the full light* is but the reflected glimmer of medieval Muslim scholars, men who themselves were believers and, therefore, of necessity, apologists.

I am sure that you have heard it said that September 11 changed America forever. That is a given, but nowhere do we hear a definitive and coherent explanation of just what, exactly, changed. What changed other than the fact that we, Americans, were attacked on our own soil? Was that for the first time in American history we have been forced to confront an Islamic militancy that has been assaulting the rest of the world for more than fourteen centuries?

This advice is taken from the article by Michael Medved on August 16, 2006, "Does U.S. Bigotry Cause Muslim Madness?"

> The best way to respond to aggressive, triumphalist religiosity from the Muslim community isn't to insist on more tolerance, or even acceptance, of Islamic demands; nor can we hope to counteract the allure of Jihadist ideology with ringing affirmations of easy-going secularism.

Given the deep-seated human hunger for connection with a supreme being, the nearly universal yearning to draw closer to eternal truth, it's not possible to beat something (radical Islam) with nothing (secular agnosticism). In this sense, the United States, with our robust movement of Christian revival, counts as far better equipped for the struggle ahead than our European allies where traditional faith of all kinds (except for Islam) has largely collapsed. Even skeptics and nonbelievers ought to welcome the vigor of Christian evangelism as the most effective counterweight to fundamentalist Islam. If those three British bomb plot suspects who converted to Islam had instead found their way to Pentecostal Christianity, or traditional Catholicism, or the Church of Jesus Christ, Latter-Day Saints, would they ever have considered killing themselves to blow planes out of the sky?

The problem with Muslim communities in the United States and Europe isn't that they face discrimination from their neighbors; it's that they receive dysfunctional, delusional teaching in too many of their own mosques. And the way to overcome that teaching isn't to demand more respect from infidel nonbelievers, but to respond to the Islamic challenge with an energetic assertion of more positive and productive religious alternatives.

This assassination of our American character is indicative of the need to free ourselves from the grip of Enlightenment conspirators, secular humanists, atheistic humanists, and others who have replaced our Christian attitude and strength in this country with a system of morals and philosophy which is, in the words of Winston Churchill, "as malevolent as Christianity was benevolent, which, if not arrested would shatter irretrievably all that Christianity has rendered possible." This malignant worldview "has been the mainspring of every subversive movement during the nineteenth century. This worldwide conspiracy for the overthrow of civilization and the reconstitution of society on the basis of arrested development, of envious malevolence, and impossible equality has been steadily growing."

CHAPTER 6

— ∽ —

Individualism

Lost Ingredient of the American Character

Christianity teaches individualism as seen in the radical command of Jesus Christ to love God totally with heart and soul and mind and strength. The second commandment is to love one's neighbor as oneself, and as such can only be sustained through courage and with a unique blend of faith and freedom. It is only the second commandment, because what makes sin most heinous in the first place is its offensiveness to God. God is always the most offended party. It follows then that the first sin is the failure to love God totally with heart and soul and mind and strength. There is more to the definition of individualism and how it is linked to Christianity and why collectivists see it as evil. In part the answer is revealed in the way the world counts time: Before Christ (BC) and Anno Domini (AD). Before Christ (BC), the collectivization and/or *oneness* of pagan pantheism ruled the world. The importance of the individual began when the God of the Bible led the Hebrews out of bondage to the Egyptians. With the actions that followed, the Hebrews virtually paved the way for the birth of Jesus Christ.

Christianity and the *individualism* that naturally occurs from belief in God as the supreme being is the primary ingredient of the American character and the stumbling block that gives rise to an intense dislike of the very word by Darwin's followers.

The Christian idea of vocation, that unique role that each Christian plays in the cosmic drama of creation and redemption, is the one root of the Western idea of individualism. It was not, in its origins, a matter of self-constituting autonomy but of living out the singular, God-given destiny that is every human life.

Here is a quote from John Dewey, the father of progressive education: "Teaching children to read was a perversion and high literacy rates bred the sustaining force behind individualism."

Dewey, in his attempts to subvert modern education along with modern civilization, has manipulated language in such a way as to lull an unsuspecting population into a stupor of compliance with tyranny. One of the key terms foisted on the masses is *individuality*, a centerpiece of progressive, socialist educational theory. Dewey argued that the *old individualism* presumes that individual human beings exist independently of their social relations, and that society is the product of the voluntary associations of individuals, the authoritarian and progressive state. This is classical liberalism or Marxism. The individual is a product of social relations: God, family, country. This is totally the opposite of individuality. Dewey's idea of the development of the individual completely denies principles of metaphysics, ethics, psychology, and logic and proclaims that without preexisting social structures, there are no individuals. Dewey believed that the collective is the primary reality, from which *individuals* may or may not develop. Dewey also believed that only socialism could produce fully realized individuals.

The following are some of Dewey's typical expressions of his view of individualism and individuality.

Liberty is that secure release and fulfillment of potentialities which take place only in rich and manifold association with others: the power to be an individualized self, making a distinctive contribution and enjoying in its own way the fruits of association (*The Essential Dewey*, Vol. 1, p. 295). Translated from the abstractions of Newspeak into English, "individuality" means striving to make oneself interesting and useful to the collective, on the collective's terms and without rocking the social boat except in the name of strengthening the social uniformity that allows the aims of authoritarian

socialism to flow "naturally" from the practice of absolute majority rule. Individuality means "active" conformity to the collective, as
indicated as early as 1899 in one of Dewey's more lucid critiques of
non-progressive education:

> The mere absorbing of facts and truths is
> so individual an affair [in the "old" sense of indi-
> vidual] that it tends very naturally to pass into
> selfishness. There is no objective social motive
> for the acquirement of mere learning, there is no
> clear social gain in success thereat. (The School
> and Society, p. 11)

By any standard, the development of the individual mind and
character now has become the enemy of the Left or the enemy of the
collective's interests or of *objective social motives*. What then is the purpose of education? What we see today on the college campuses is the
result of atheistic humanism and diversity that is spoon-fed by leftist,
progressive intellectual professors for the purpose of anarchy. This is
the type of *true democracy* Dewey wanted to establish. Reminiscent of
G. K. Chesterton and the "old ship," all the students of today want to
do is tear down the "old ship." They take to the streets, confused and
not sure of their purpose of demonstration. They go through protesting with zombie-like improvisation and as a system of mass indoctrination. It does not matter what they are protesting. Individualism is,
to begin with, an ethical position based on a rational understanding
of human nature and the virtues that follow from it as the Creator
intended. The goal of higher education is no longer learning but
social activism and anarchy. There is no place for virtue in the world
of the collective good which glorifies the collective and debases the
individual. There can be no distinction of gender any longer, and
manliness and its virtues are without portfolio. We now fight battles
about which bathroom to use simply because a small percentage of
people wake up each day confused as to whether they want to be
male or female. The crux of the matter comes into view as individualism encourages proper pride and self-reliance; approval may come

as it may, but it can never be the primary motive of genuine virtue. Individuality, on the contrary, is defined by an emotional need for approval and acceptance. One stands out precisely in order to be noticed, to be applauded, to be more fully and actively immersed in the collective and its majoritarian will. Ronald Reagan exemplifies individualism; Barack Obama, the historically cool socialist, is the definition of individuality.

It may be said that this *new individualism* has won the day. In one sense, it is profoundly correct to say that individualism is an adult ethic, individuality essentially childish. This should not come as a big surprise, in light of the fact that individuality has been created and propped up by authoritarians, with a view to reducing their subjects to a compliant mass of obedient, needy, trusting dependents.

America had very high literacy rates prior to Dewey's progressive system of education. This was seen as a threat to their real purpose which was and is to create a socialist world order. To achieve these goals, it is necessary to remove from the minds of men their individualism, loyalty to family traditions, national patriotism, and religious dogma. This is a statement from The World Federation of Mental Health:

> Every child in America entering school at the age of five is mentally ill because he comes to school with certain allegiances to our Founding Fathers, toward our elected officials, toward his parents, toward a belief in a supernatural being, and toward the sovereignty of this nation as a separate entity. It's up to you as teachers to make all these sick children well—by creating the international child of the future." (Chester Pierce, Professor of Education and Psychiatry at Harvard 1970)

G. K. Chesterton, in a vision of allegory with his book *The Ball and the Cross,* clearly intends a mirror reflection of the conflict between the church, the individual, and Satan. It is a conflict that will continue until the end of time or until the return of Jesus Christ.

William F. Buckley, in the introduction to a reprinting of his first book *God and Man at Yale*, wrote, "The duel between Christianity and atheism is the most important in the world. I further believe that the struggle between individualism and collectivism is the same struggle reproduced on a higher level."

Individualism, as opposed to collectivism, is the concept that all values, rights, and duties originate in individuals. It goes without saying that all men are created equal, that they are endowed by their Creator with certain unalienable rights. Among these are *life, liberty, and the pursuit of happiness*. These values, rights, and duties are part of man's soul at the time of his creation.

While Tocqueville believed individualism to be a vice, he was speaking of the secular form of individualism and not the command of Christianity to love your neighbor as yourself. There is in Tocqueville's writing the idea of the American enterprise being a collective individualism.

Individuals coming together in a collective effort is called organization, and it is essential in striving to build that city upon the hill. There are times when individuals must put aside their personal interests and sacrifice for the good of the whole community.

The disappearance of individual freedoms will happen when collective, fanatical views from either side of the conflict captures a nation and promotes tyranny. Check out that Communion of Saints, Ted Kennedy, Charles Schumer, Patrick Leahy, Harry Reid, and Nancy Pelosi.

It is the individual who makes the choice to accept Jesus Christ as Lord and Savior. It is the individual who makes the choice and professes that faith through baptism before and within a community and through the power and wisdom of the Holy Spirit to know the truth and the fellowship of faith-minded individuals, who make up the *body of Christ*. It is at that moment that you join the *community of Christ*, and it is the individual who faces the reality of his own mortality. It is the individual who chooses how free will is exercised.

And when the time comes for you to stand before God on your day of judgment, you will be alone and He will judge you as an individual responsible for your own actions. God will not accept the plea that you were a victim of the ills of society.

Agendas with a common link. This common link is the only way that all Americans may view this agenda-driven society controlled by evolutionary secular humanism and atheistic humanism. The evil of this system is that they seek to gain power through the reversal of human norms, natural law, and the social institutions so necessary for the continuance of mankind and freedom and democracy in the United States of America. It is a malignancy-filled system of philosophy comparable to a *grimoire of goetia* or black magic.

The goal of all of these agendas from the left-wing liberal critique is the same. It is the destruction of individualism and the individual's belief in the one true radical doctrine of Christianity "to love your neighbor as yourself." That is the goal of all of the agendas who are claiming in the name of the progressive (liberal) spirit seeking further progress toward social justice.

People like Noam Chomsky and Howard Zinn believe that nation-states are merely a fiction, and only economic classes are *real* social actors. His signature book, *A Peoples History of the United States*, is a poorly conceived Marxist version of the United States of America that begins with Columbus and ends with George Bush. His historical method was a political agenda relieved of objectivity, and his intent was to view American history as a conspiracy of rich White men to oppress and exploit *the people*.

Most, but not all, of the progressives share similar goals. They want to make politics more democratic, business more responsible, society more moral and more just. They have been deeply affected by Darwinism and biblical criticism and began to exhibit a secular outlook generally. Progressivism may be understood as one of the secular revival movements of American history, but it is a revival in which individuals exhibited feelings of guilt over their social behavior rather than over their purely personal or private relationships. They have chosen to relinquish, in a quest for salvation, their personal relationship with their Creator and instead seek salvation in a social rather than the Christian ideal of individualism. There is within the soul of the people a conviction of their past unrighteousness.

Nationalism in America, as in Europe or most of Europe, meant both nationalism and socialism. Edward Bellamy explained in his novel from 1888, *Looking Backward*, that America has finally created the kingdom of heaven on earth. Indeed, everyone looks back on *the age of individualism* with bemused contempt. The story was set in the year 2000, and everyone lived in a utopian, militarized society. This has been suggested as the starting date for the progressive race for the Great Society.

The Progressive Party convention of 1912 was a blend of scientific utopianism, nationalism, socialism, and Christianity. The American social gospel and Christian sociology movements in essence sought to bend Christianity to the progressive social agenda. The left-wing clergy were convinced that the state was the instrument of God and that collectivism was the new order sanctioned by Jesus. Conservative theologians argued that only the individual could be born again. Progressive Christians claimed that individuals no longer mattered and that only the state could serve as the medium in their search for the kingdom of God. Richard Ely, who was a mentor to Woodrow Wilson and a great influence on Teddy Roosevelt, insisted that the state "is religious in its essence" and that there is no element of human existence beyond the authority of the state.

Following World War II, liberalism began to see the need for a unifying philosophy. They found that the orthodox Marxist narrative was largely falling on deaf ears and was unpersuasive to the masses. The Frankfurt School, comprised of a handful of immensely influential Marxist theorists, found the glue they needed in psychology. This union between Marxism and psychology provided a new vocabulary for liberalism. Nazism and fascism were seen as and described as mass psychosis. That analysis is not hard to digest, but they continued to elaborate with the notion that since Marxism is far superior objectively to its alternatives, anyone who disagrees must be quite mad.

Richard Hofstadter, the Columbia University historian, was to become the leading proponent of Theodor Adorno's book *The Authoritarian Personality*. In his book, Adorno found that it was easier to dismiss the conservative mind by simply defining it in psychiatric terms and to show liberal intellectuals how to conduct political criticism in psychiatric categories and to make those categories bear the weight of political criticism. Using the tactics of Adorno, Hofstadter was free of the difficult task of judgment and argumentation. He was content to use psychological scare words as he did in his book *The Paranoid Style in American Politics*. Hofstadter quotes Adorno in his book from 1965 on page 44, *Part I: Studies in the American Right*, the pseudo-conservative shows "conventionality and authoritarian submissiveness" in his conscious thinking and "violence, anarchic impulses, and chaotic destructiveness in the unconscious sphere... The pseudo-conservative is a man who, in the name of upholding traditional American values and institutions and defending them against more or less fictitious dangers, consciously or unconsciously aims at their abolition."

Modern psychology became the all-purpose solution for the progressive's quest to find the perfect substitute for their religion of government. They were now able to direct their energies toward and upon the psychologically unfit. With *The Authoritarian Personality*, Adorno and his fellow Marxist theorists laid the groundwork for the transition by identifying the *authoritarian family* as the focal point and stated conditions for evil in the modern world.

Progressivism (liberalism and/or liberal democrats) brought new interest in replacing religion with the state in modern society as a progressive doctrine of state sovereignty. Progressivism implies a collective society the same as socialism. It raises many more questions on the nature of America and American liberty. American liberty was built solidly upon respect for the individual and upon almost universal devotion to the laws of nature and nature's god. Collectivism, on the other hand, is anti-liberty and anti-American. Human freedom can only subsist in political and social communities that value the individual.

Leszek Kolakowski in a paper he delivered defining his reasons for rejecting his long-held beliefs, "My Correct Ideas on Everything" exposes the double standards that are crucial to the arguments used by the Left. The first of three forms of the double standard is the invocation of moral standards in judging capitalist regimes, while historical criteria are used to evaluate their socialist counterparts.

Secondly, capitalist and socialist regimes are always judged differently when discussing and assessing their futures. Capitalist systems were seen as stagnate and unable to improve, and yet the socialist regimes were always judged on the assumption that they would improve. Repressions by conservative governments were never seen as necessary preludes to democratic restorations but were condemned as unmitigated evils. However, far greater repressions of revolutionary regimes and dictatorships are minimized as just that, necessary steps along the path to a progressive future.

The third form of the double standard is that the negative aspects of existing socialism are always attributed to capitalist influences. There are usually elements of the previous or old society that remain. Did Hitler give rise to Stalinism or was it the other way around? It would seem more likely that the socialist assault on democracy and the example of the forced labor camps gave impetus to Nazism.

It is not the *dialectical materialism* of Marxism, for as an economic policy that is dead, or at least it was until the Obama administration began reviving it, but Marxism as a social philosophy has never been more popular. Its goal is the destruction of Western civilization, which is generally described as a hierarchical, heterosexual, White, Christian, patriarchal, capitalistic system of oppression. You must belong to the proper victim group, or your opposition to this neo-Marxism will be properly dismissed.

Our individualism is that unique blend of faith and freedom that provides us with a wall that is impregnable as long as we continue to defend our individualism and strengthen that blend of faith and freedom—faith in the form of Judeo Christian values and identity. We cannot afford to lose that identity and faith. Once that happens, this nation is doomed.

CHAPTER 7

───── ✍ ─────

Militant Christianity and the
American Character

"Any leader who comes with armed support in the name of a compelling faith, is sure of a following." For Charlemagne, that faith was chivalry or militant Christianity, "the most powerful [faith] the world has ever seen."

It is time for a rebirth of chivalry. In this treatise it will be referenced as *militant Christianity* as well as chivalry. The resounding cry of "All for one and one for all" resonating from King Arthur and the Knights of the Round Table was to fight and defend the weak against the strong. Today it is the duty of every Christian to rise up and defend against those who wish to destroy Western culture, the Bill of Rights, and our constitution. Chivalry is an important ingredient of the American character. It is seen as a vital commandment to each and every American who is imbued with the spirit that is our constitution. To stand and defend the weak against the strong. To obey the command of the Savior "to love God with heart and soul and mind and strength, to love thy neighbor as thyself." This is the radical command of Jesus Christ. It is time to take a stand.

The need for *militant Christianity* is not a supercilious notion coming from the *right-wing radical nuts* as the Left tends to label anyone who believes in God and is of the Christian faith, but it is in response to the drift away from any sociological, as well as theological, moorings.

There can no longer be a body of people who refuse to take a stand in the face of moral decay. Those who would allow secular corruption of our children by not allowing prayer in school, by not allowing the Ten Commandments to be displayed, by proclaiming that any display of the birth of Christ in the form of a manger scene on the courthouse lawn or public school grounds or any public property is an establishment of religion are wrong and deliberate in their intent.

We can no longer be tolerant of judges and politicians who wish to destroy our constitution and our reliance on old identities. They must be revitalized and reaffirmed, not blurred and compromised. We, as Christians, in order to survive, need to rediscover theological firmness and doctrinal clarity.

The liberal Left refuses to acknowledge that our unity arises from an ideology and value system that is more right of center than they are willing to admit, but we continue to sleepwalk while our culture is being systematically destroyed from within.

It is imperative that we free ourselves from the grip of progressives, liberals, and Enlightenment conspirators, secular humanists, who have attempted to replace our Christian attitude and strength in this country, as they have in Europe, with a system of morals and philosophy which, in the words of Winston Churchill, is "as malevolent as Christianity was benevolent, which, if not arrested would shatter irretrievably all that Christianity has rendered possible."

This malignant worldview "has been the mainspring of every subversive movement during the nineteenth century. This worldwide conspiracy for the overthrow of civilization and the reconstitution of society on the basis of arrested development, of envious malevolence, and impossible equality has been steadily growing."

There is a sense of meaninglessness and disorder that has been growing since the nineteenth century. From the writings of Friedrich Nietzsche, "At last the horizon lies free before us, even granted that it is not bright; at least the sea, our sea, lies open before us. Perhaps there has never been so open a sea." The sum of this philosophy is to reject the idea that the world has been created by God for a purpose or that it is the self-manifestation of the absolute idea or spirit. This rejection sets man free to develop the meaning of life that he sees fit or wills to give it. And it has no other meaning. It is an absence of morality and grace as fostered by Rousseau and the French in the eighteenth century.

Diversity and moral relativism, where no idea is superior to another, are dangerous metaphors for division, confusion, and mediocrity. College students fall prey to what G. K. Chesterton said about people, "When people stop believing in God, they don't believe in nothing, they believe in anything."

Social justice agendas were launched in the name of civil rights and other rights that exist only in the minds of nine justices of the Supreme Court who were never elected to any legislative office and with the sole purpose of creating in America a cultural revolution in which God no longer dominates the moral horizon and personal autonomy and individual choice become the twin pillars of a debased moral view.

The ACLU and their theology of atheistic humanism (social Darwinism in disguise) is attempting to gain power through the reversal of human norms, natural law, and the social institutions that are so necessary for the continuance of mankind and our republican form of government.

Agendas with a common link. The ACLU, gay rights agenda, feminism with their agenda, the right of a woman to have control over her reproductive system through abortion, and there are far too many more agendas to mention, but the common link is always there. This is the manner in which we must view this agenda-driven society controlled by evolutionary secular humanism. The evil of this system is that they seek to gain power through the reversal of human norms, natural law, and the social institutions so necessary for the continuance of mankind and freedom and democracy in the Republic of the United States of America. It is a malignancy-filled system of philosophy comparable to a *grimoire of goetia* or black magic.

The gay rights agenda is a prime example of how a small percentage of the population, through a carefully crafted and decades-old propaganda campaign, has carefully and successfully portrayed homosexuals as a disadvantaged minority. Their goal is the same as previously stated regarding the ACLU, the feminist movement, human rights campaign, the National Education Association and their Darwinian approach of social indoctrination. It is not the education of our children, nor civil rights for those who truly need help that they are concerned about, but the destruction of Christianity, promoting of socialism and collectivism and the destruction of our republic, through the reversal of human norms, natural law, and the social institutions that have been defined by thousands of years of history. They have repackaged and sold to the American public a new definition of behavior that is by all standards identified as immoral and sexually deviant. It is moral relativism applied to sexual morality, and the purpose is to replace all traditional forms of right and wrong and all notions of sexual morality with a post-modern idea of sexual relativism.

Marshall Kirk and Hunter Madsen, in their marketing manuscript of 1989, *After the Ball*, very carefully and very succinctly laid out the homosexual lobby's blueprint for success in what is widely considered to be the handbook for the gay agenda. In it they provide a three-pronged attack for silencing Christians: 1) desensitizing; 2) jamming; and finally 3) conversion. Their goal is to create cultural and moral anarchy.

Matt Barber, who works with Concerned Women for America, has outlined the plan of attack in his article published on February 13, 2008. Unmasking the gay agenda requires that you understand that they are very affirmative in principle. By force of law, with Hate Crimes Legislation and other acts such as Employment Non-Discrimination Act (ENDA), they intend to demand comprehensive acceptance of homosexual conduct. The courts have ignored the voters and will of the people and imposed government-sanctioned *same-sex marriage* by declaring such laws and definition of marriage as unconstitutional. People, and the traditional values they hold, are directly in the cross hairs of official government policy. According to the homosexual lobby, their primary objective is to gain power through the reversal of human norms, natural law, and the social and foundational institutions that are so necessary for the continuance of marriage, the nuclear family, God's natural design for mankind and human sexuality. These are the same principles that guide the progressive and/or liberal politics and politicians. Their desire is to create a spiritual and biological world in which the natural distinctions between male and female are dissolved. They wish to create a sexually androgynous society having both male and female characteristics.

Gay activists are now headed for the churches. They want to *celebrate diversity*, so now they demand that their abnormal behaviors not only be tolerated but celebrated. They have hidden their true agenda and have employed the rhetoric of the Civil Rights movement with such phrases as *tolerance* and *diversity*. Anyone who does not approve of this behavior by homosexuals is branded *homophobic* or *hatemonger* and are to be silenced.

The 1972 Gay Rights Platform reveals two of the central demands of, as Matt Barber describes them, "the homosexual lobby's lavender curtain."

One, "Repeal all laws governing the age of sexual consent." As you can see, this opens up our children and teens to pedophiles and homosexuals who wish to prey on them.

Two, "Repeal all legislative provisions that restrict the sex or number of persons entering into a marriage unit." This is an all-out attempt to redefine marriage so that all objections to any conceivable combination are rendered with having no practical significance.

During the 1987 March on Washington, the homosexual lobby put forth more demands: the government should provide protection from discrimination based on sexual orientation in employment, public accommodations, and education just as protection is provided on race, creed, color, sex, or national origin. This is the so-called ENDA, and it would have the effect of forcing all religious business owners, landlords, and schools to abandon sincerely held and constitutionally protected beliefs and adopt the homosexual view of sexual morality which seems to be entirely counter to the central teachings of Christianity and of every major world religion.

Recently, the governor of Colorado signed into law a bill passed by the legislature to outlaw gender-specific restrooms and locker rooms statewide. This *transgender nondiscrimination* bill makes it illegal to deny a person access to public accommodations, including restrooms and locker rooms based on gender identity or the perception of *gender* identity. The Supreme Court, in recent decisions, has shown a propensity to base their decisions on, in the words of Justice Kennedy, "evolving standards of decency that mark the progress of a maturing society" or, should we say, *indecency.*

Their list of demands expands daily, and the arenas of attack multiply as well. Primarily, the churches are in peril, and while it is the duty of the church to minister to those outside of the fold, how does the church keep from being used as the instrument of approval for the homosexual lifestyle? This is part of the gay agenda: to change the foundational beliefs of the Christian church and force the church to ordain openly gay ministers. The biblically conservative churches provide the most difficult target for the gay agenda, especially if the believers stress that the practice of homosexuality is incompatible with Christian teaching.

Regardless of the best intentions of the Christian faith to minister to the homosexual in need of redemption, there is a tone of intimidation in the tactics of the gay religious activists. This is the danger the Christian church faces in attempting to minister to the aberrant theology and practices of the gay community. Their goal is not to change their lifestyle but to force us to accept their lifestyle. It is a blatant attempt to play the pity card.

Finally, Kirk and Madsen have devised a three-pronged plan that the homosexual lobby has implemented with full force and fury: desensitization, jamming, and conversion. These approaches are meant to: 1) portray gays as victims, not as aggressive challengers; 2) give potential protectors a just cause; 3) make gays look good; 4) make victimizers look bad. Desensitization means that if we cannot shut off the shower, maybe at least we will get used to being wet. Jamming refers to the public smearing of Christians, traditionalists, or anyone who opposes the gay agenda or anyone who holds traditional values regarding human sexuality as Nazis, Klansmen, homophobes, and too many other names to mention. Conversion is the most devious of the three due to the medium used for the "conversion of the average American's emotions, mind, and will, through a planned psychological attack, in the form of propaganda fed to the nation via the media."

Alexander King, who used to be a regular on the Jack Parr late-night TV show, used to say that the American people were so gullible that they would buy "sheep dip kumquats" if the marketing people presented them as though they were a delicacy. Sadly, he was very insightful. The arrogant, self-serving liberal media is probably our greatest enemy. It is time to take a stand.

CHAPTER 8

———— ⟡ ————

Judicial Activism as a Form of Moral Relativism

Woodrow Wilson, with his liberal progressive agenda, pioneered the doctrine of a *living constitution* that today's liberals and as far back as Wilson and the *New Deal* of Franklin Roosevelt were using as the basis for their transformation of American politics. Wilson believed that the individual had no meaning apart from the society in which his individuality had been formed. Wilson and those progressives who followed him later on believed that freedom did not come from nature or from God but is instead a product of the state and is realized only in the modern state. By removing the absolutes, liberalism has led to a reversal of human norms and natural law while, without knowing and with indifference, we have fallen into a wilderness of *moral relativism and moral equivalency.*

Diversity and moral relativism, where no idea is superior to another, are dangerous metaphors for division, confusion, and mediocrity. College students fall prey to what G. K. Chesterton said about the world of atheism, "When people stop believing in God, they don't believe in nothing, they believe in anything."

Following the communist collapse, the great majority of the secular progressive intellectuals continued their war against the democracies of the West and are now professors teaching in some of the finest universities and colleges in the Western Hemisphere.

They continue their destructive attacks on capitalism believing that the collapse of communism was the fault of those who attempted its reform. Many or most of them never seem to confront the moral issue posed by their destructive agendas.

"The explicit agenda of critical theory is to undermine the credibility and authority of the status quo in order to prepare its annihilation." Critical theory is the coy self-description of the ideological Left. It defines itself by the totality of its rejection of the existing social order.

Earl Warren, over the course of his life, came to value freedom more highly and to see security not as undermined by freedom but rather as its product. Must liberty be curtailed in order to preserve the nation, or is the nation better understood as an expression of its freedoms? No, it is better understood as an expression of its character, the American character. And if the American character is diminished or forsaken, then so are our freedoms. Liberty then becomes only a memory. The Warren Court never understood this, and I am not convinced that some of the current justices could ever understand this line of thought either.

The Warren Court, and especially the chief justice, was determined in the middle 1960s to fashion the "clearest expression of Warren's America, the America that he had spent his life fashioning and that he now had the license and authority to recast in his terms." Mistakenly, Warren and his court thought that they could create *an enforced code of decency* through the Supreme Court, and with time, "the Court would stake out and clarify its revolutionary principles of jurisprudence and of American society."

Racial equality evolved into a sweeping commitment to egalitarianism. All of this is nothing more than *social engineering*, and with it comes Supreme Court decisions based on: 1) Warren's own conscience and the mistakes and injustices of his early career in California, the feelings of guilt he harbored from the internment of the Japanese and the part he played in the incarceration of an innocent people; and 2) in his attempt to promote fairness and equality, Warren Court was forged from his compassion and his idea of social justice and not from the rule of law. Archibald Cox described the appointment of Earl Warren as chief justice of the United States in 1953 as the moment that marked a new era in the nation's constitutional development. It was the Warren Court of Social Justice. Constitutional decision as an instrument of social reform. During the next fifteen years, the Supreme Court under Earl Warren totally rewrote, with profound social consequences, major constitutional doctrines governing race relations, the administration of criminal justice, and the operation of the political process. The extent and the rapidity of these changes raise grave questions concerning the nature and function of constitutional adjudication and the proper role of the Supreme Court in the national life. There was never any consideration given to the victims of crime, only to the so-called fair treatment of the criminal and his rights. Our liberty is at stake, the American character is being attacked, and our nation is weakened because of the ideal of Earl Warren that came to value freedom more highly and to see security not as undermined by freedom but rather as its product. Our institutions are a product of our economic and social conditions, an expression of our character, the American character. It is the American character that protects our liberty and our freedoms. Democracy—sound democracy and the republic, its rule by law and reliance on principles that do not change—is not a cause but an effect of our national character—character in the leaders of our institutions, both economic and social, and character in our people. Our character is defined by the statement "In God We Trust." This we must never forget, that America is a secular nation in its political foundation, and it is also a powerful religious idea in implementation and in character. Christianity has played a very big role in the formation of the American character.

This Day in Liberal Judicial Activism—May 23 [Ed Whelan]

1957—Three Cleveland police officers arrive at Dolly Mapp's home seeking a suspect wanted in connection with a recent bombing. After Mapp refuses to admit them, the police forcibly enter and search the home and discover

obscene materials. Mapp is convicted of possession of these materials. The Ohio Supreme Court
rules that the search of the home was unlawful
but that Mapp's conviction resting on evidence
resulting from the search is valid.

In *Mapp v. Ohio* (1961), the Supreme Court, by a vote of 5
to 3, overrules its own 1949 precedent that held that the constitution does *not* require that evidence obtained in violation of the constitution be excluded from criminal trials in state court. The court
instead applies to state criminal trials the exclusionary rule that it first
imposed on federal criminal trials in 1914. In dissent, Justice Harlan
(joined by Justices Frankfurter and Whittaker) concludes his analysis
with this observation: "I regret that I find so unwise in principle and
so inexpedient in policy a decision motivated by the high purpose of
increasing respect for constitutional rights. But in the last analysis I
think this Court can increase respect for the constitution only if it
rigidly respects the limitations which the constitution places upon it,
and respects as well the principles inherent in its own processes. In
the present case I think we exceed both, and that our voice becomes
only a voice of power, not of reason."

The dissent by Justices Harlan, Frankfurter, and Whittaker
shines a spotlight on the Warren Court and the chief justice in particular as a destructive force in American life and respect for the
constitution. I believe Justice Harlan's analysis reflects the truth of
the Founding Fathers when he says, "I think this Court can increase
respect for the constitution only if it rigidly respects the limitations
which the constitution places upon it, and respects as well the principles inherent in its own processes." This change in direction, set
in motion by the Warren Court and its liberal judicial activism, has
been the single most mendacious attack on the text of the constitution and the American character. It was true to Warren's nature
that the voice of the Court became only a voice of power and not of
reason.

CHAPTER 9

Woodrow Wilson and the Sources of Progressivism

The Destruction of the American Character

Where is the Democratic Party of Woodrow Wilson and his liberal progressive politics today? It is hidden in the liberal agendas of administrations that include Franklin D. Roosevelt. The New Deal, John F. Kennedy, while not a modern liberal himself, after his death was turned into a martyr for the religion of the *great society* of Lyndon Johnson, during whose administration the gulf within our culture began to widen. America began to come apart at the seams, the neo-pagan pantheism of Al Gore *(Earth in the Balance)* and the late Ted Kennedy who proclaimed liberty for all Americans and yet saw fit to *grant* liberty only to those who espouse these same liberal agendas by advocating the passage of social legislation in the Supreme Court rather than through the Congress, the people's voice. Their idea of liberty is the power to dispense liberty through government as they (those in power) see fit, while denying liberty to those who form the vast majority of Americans. Liberalism in its most pernicious form is now seen in the administration of Barack Obama, whose idea of governing is distinctly fascistic and totalitarian. It is called anarchy.

They claim that they want to change America and they do—remember the Langston Hughes 1938 poem "Let America be America again"—but not for the better or for the good. They seek to change America to their own liking. They are intent on creating a whole new system of morality, a morality based on moral relativism and tolerance. Traditional morality becomes a thing of the past. Once you accept this idea of tolerance as the guiding principle of the new morality, the antithesis of right and wrong no longer exists and tolerance becomes acceptance. A better term might be atheistic humanism or secular humanism. This is not the atheism of individuals who are seeking to impress or become a part of a group of intellectual elites, but atheism with a developed ideology and a program for remaking the world.

Woodrow Wilson saw the American character as moral principle endowed by God and possessive of a special providence that required finely balanced decision making while spreading the religion of American principles known as liberty, equality, and democracy. Since the early days America has considered herself marked and chosen, a nation blessed by God far beyond that which is deserved. He saw Americanism as a message to be spread in the same manner a missionary would spread the Word of God. President Wilson preached an active, chivalrous, global Americanism. This is what I first believed of Woodrow Wilson as one expression of Woodrow Wilson from a biographer who did not read deeply into Wilson's philosophy of government. Reading from Wilson's own writings you find a different story. In a collection of speeches delivered during his campaign for president and included in a collection of speeches called *The New Freedom*, Wilson puts forward his idea of an evolving or *living* constitution. Wilson believed in what Hegel called historical contingency. He states that because the laws have not kept pace with the economic and political circumstances, this country has not made progress since the beginning. This has forced him to become a progressive. Historical contingency, however, means that there are no permanent or immutable principles. Rather they are dependent upon the particular circumstances of history. While all of his rhetoric seemed to be in defense of liberty, his progressive soul caused him to believe that government was not a threat to society. Wilson believed that the real force in any society was its organic will, and government is a creature of that will.

Wilson stated that "Liberty has never come from the government. Liberty has always come from the subjects of the government. The history of government is a history of resistance. The history of liberty is the history of the limitation of government, not the increase of it." The fact is you must not let his words cloud his actions. He speaks of liberty while promoting a collective philosophy that states that the people exercise their rights in a collective environment, an environment created by government. Wilson, in his speeches collectively entitled *The New Freedom*, stated that government is not a machine, but a living thing. "It falls, not under the theory of the universe, but under the theory of organic life. It is accountable to Darwin, not to Newton. It is modified by its environment, necessitated by its tasks, shaped to its functions by sheer pressure of life. No living thing can have its organs offset against each other, as checks, and live. On the contrary, its life is dependent upon their quick cooperation, their ready response to the commands of instinct or intelligence, their amicable community of purpose. There can be no successful government without the intimate, instinctive coordination of the organs of life and action. This is not theory, but fact, and displays its force as fact, whatever theories may be thrown across its track. Living political constitutions must be Darwinian in structure and in practice. Society is a living organism and must obey the laws of life, not of mechanics; it must develop." He continues with the progressive line of thought to interpret the constitution according to the Darwinian principle.

In this case you have to understand the subversion of modern education and of modern civilization.

There is an absence of truth and honor in what they say and do in today's Democratic Party. President Wilson was quoting one day to some of his colleagues in the Senate some lines from Shakespeare's "Henry V" which had always appealed to him: "If it be a sin to covet honor, then am I the most offending soul alive."

He went on to say that he coveted honor for the great party of which he was a member, because that party is not honorable unless it redeems its name and serves the people of the United States. Is this the Democratic Party of today? I think not. When you come right down to the basics, it is all about honor and character, the American character.

David Gelernter, in his book *Americanism: The Fourth Great Western Religion*, has argued that:

1) America is not only a nation; America is a religious idea;
2) America is a biblical (not secular) republic. Americanism is a biblical (not civil) religion;
3) America and Americanism were shaped by Christianity, especially Puritan Christianity; and
4) Puritan Christianity was shaped by the Bible, especially the Hebrew Bible.

That idea of *liberty, equality, and democracy* is the basis of Gelernter's *American Creed*, one of the two basic components of the American religion. The other component being that Puritanism laid out the basis of Americanism by developing American Zionism and other essential ingredients of the American religion.

American Zionism is the doctrine that was refined by the revolutionary generation. The Puritan colonists had long dreamed of liberty, equality, and democracy, and now they saw these human rights as crucially important. The colonists were made to believe that they were being oppressed by England and George III just as Israel had been oppressed by Egypt and led out of Egypt by Moses. It was an updated version of biblical principles from the Old Testament that basically and through the dynamics of the revolutionary generation created not only a new nation but created a new dynamic in the world's spiritual history.

George Weigel makes a bold proposition that maybe the possibility of reading history a very old-fashioned way, St. Augustine's way, "through lenses ground by the tools of theology" might provide answers that have yet to be fully explained by the political or psychological.

Barbara Tuchman outlines the miscalculations and destructive passions that brought Europe and the continent to war in 1914 in "The Guns of August." The fact that the German, French, English, and Russian general staffs had their war plans completed at least ten years before hostilities began is an indication of the growing paranoia that existed on the European continent. Mrs. Tuchman revealed the human reasons for the disasters of war that unfolded. Others saw it as a crisis of civilizational morality. The currents of history may need to search for a deeper explanation. Depravity of culture and morals will render society helpless when they are godless.

Aleksandr Solzhenitsyn claims that it happened and continued to happen because men had forgotten God. Solzhenitsyn was a moralist and was strongly allied against *moral relativism*; he readily defends the time honored distinctions between good and evil and truth and falsehood. He sees the decline of civilizational morality beginning with the Great War, World War I of 1914–1918. His novel, *August 1914*, is an example of his genius in combining art, history, and politics in a social and historic panorama.

It was not balance of power politics that led the world into the madness; it was the product of a crisis of civilizational morality, a failure of moral reason in a culture that had given the world the very concept of moral reason.

Woodrow Wilson took America into the first World War after a long struggle for neutrality ended. Woodrow Wilson's name has been linked to a group who were actively molding foreign policy long before Wilson moved to Washington and before he became president. The school of thought some called *idealist* foreign policy was misleading. This eventually became known as the Wilsonian school of foreign policy. It must be noted, however, that the ideas and principles that underlie this school of thought are more deeply rooted in the national character and deeply related to the national interest upon further examination.

Wilson was a man of many paradoxes. Some would say that for Wilson to be successful in politics was indeed remarkable, for he lacked the necessary practical qualities. He was after all a man of personal and intellectual distinction. Woodrow Wilson, with his liberal progressive agenda, pioneered the doctrine of a living constitution that today's liberals and as far back as Wilson and the New Deal of Franklin Roosevelt were using as the basis for their transformation of American politics, individual liberty, and the American character. The liberal progressives of Wilson and Roosevelt believed in statism. Wilson believed that the individual had no meaning apart from the society in which his individuality (as distinguished from individualism) had been formed. Wilson and those progressives who followed him later on believed that freedom did not come from nature or from God but is instead a product of the state and is realized only in the modern state. By removing the absolutes, liberalism has led to a reversal of human norms and natural law while, without knowing and with indifference, we have fallen into a wilderness of *moral relativism*.

In his new book, *Liberal Fascism*, Jonah Goldberg expounds the theory and offers proof by definition that during the Wilson administration the United States was being mobilized as a fascist state. Fascism is generally considered militaristic because militarism was progressive in the early part of the twentieth century. It is the organizing principle for mobilizing society, and as William James had stated, it is the moral equivalent of war.

Herbert Croly, as the editor of *The New Republic*, pushed relentlessly for war and hoped that war "should bring with it a political and economic organization better able to redeem its obligations at home." Walter Lippmann promised that hostilities would bring out a "transvaluation of values as radical as anything in the history of intellect." Croly later expressed the hope that America's entry into the war would provide "the tonic of a serious moral adventure." Croly also was the author of a book, *The Promise of American Life*, which gave form to an idea according to Croly, whose time had come, the progressive movement, and in modern-day terms, liberalism. Croly followed up this first work with progressive democracy in 1914.

Progressivism did not begin and end with these two titles, for his most-lasting achievement may have come in 1914 when, along with Walter Lippmann and a few wealthy financial backers, helped found the new republic. Croly served as first editor of *The New Republic.*

According to Herbert Croly, "For better or worse, democracy cannot be disentangled from an aspiration toward human perfectibility, and hence from the adoption of measures looking in the direction of realizing such an aspiration."

Belief in the perfectibility of all mankind. It is a never-ending struggle of the progressive mind and one that is truly revolutionary, but America is able to recognize her failures and continues to believe and to strive for liberty and not equality. All men are created equal by their Creator not by the state, but through freedom and liberty they are given equal opportunity to achieve their level according to their talents. The American founders had what may be called a sober view of human nature. They believed that ordinary people were quite capable of greatness and nobility, especially if given sufficient freedom. The Founding Fathers realized that even the best of people could behave badly, so the powers of government had to be strictly limited and arranged in such a way that the tyranny of either an individual or an overbearing faction would find the path to power difficult if not impossible.

Croly's argument in *The Promise of American Life* combined a simple thesis with a complex demonstration of that thesis. It is at least an echo of Comte. Progress can only be interpreted to mean movement toward greater perfection. What prevented progress toward perfected democracy in America was not the influence of simple reactionaries, important as that was, but rather two distinct strands of thought that competed against each other and had their origins in the founding principles of the regime.

The first was the Thomas Jefferson tradition of individualism and democracy.

The second was the nationalist tradition represented by the more far-sighted Alexander Hamilton, which, incidentally, was best represented in contemporary politics in the person of Ronald Reagan, but it is also a powerful religious idea in implementation and in character. Christianity has played a very big role in the formation of the American character.

The dissent by Justices Harlan, Frankfurter, and Whittaker shines a spotlight on the Warren Court and the chief justice in particular as a destructive force in American life and respect for the constitution. I believe Justice Harlan's analysis reflects the truth of the Founding Fathers when he says, "I think this Court can increase respect for the constitution only if it rigidly respects the limitations which the constitution places upon it, and respects as well the principles inherent in its own processes." This change in direction, set in motion by the Warren Court and its liberal judicial activism, has been the single most mendacious attack on the text of the constitution and the American character. It was true to Warren's nature that the voice of the court became only a voice of power and not of reason.

Theodore Roosevelt. Roosevelt combined, in Croly's view, the strong national government of Hamilton with the democratic faith of Jefferson. Roosevelt would use Hamiltonian means to achieve Jeffersonian ends. Croly saw a fundamental weakness in each of these founders. In Jefferson, it was his resistance to the growth of national power, and the weakness of Hamilton was his resistance to democracy. Excessive democratic individualism in Jefferson fought with excessive economic concentration of power in Hamilton. This tension between Jefferson and Hamilton had been the defining characteristic of American politics since the founding.

Why was Abraham Lincoln in 1862, in the middle of a civil war that was tearing the country apart, able to speak of this nation's destiny in these terms as "the last best hope of earth?" Lincoln saw the civil war as an instrument of God's justice for the sin of slavery, the true and righteous judgments of the Lord.

It is Abraham Lincoln who defines the American character and transformed it by teaching America that it should embody its noble ideals. Lincoln changed the American character at a time when, in the presence of slavery, the Declaration of Independence had lost its meaning. He changed it by leading the under Earl Warren, totally rewrote, with profound social consequences, major constitutional doctrines governing race relations, the administration of criminal justice, and the operation of the political process. The extent and the rapidity of these changes raise grave questions concerning the nature and function of constitutional adjudication and the proper role of the Supreme Court in the national life. There was never any consideration given to the victims of crime, only to the so-called fair treatment of the criminal and his rights. Our liberty is at stake, the American character is being attacked, and our nation is weakened because of the ideal of Earl Warren that came to value freedom more highly and to see security not as undermined by freedom but rather as its product. Our institutions are a product of our economic and social conditions, an expression of our character, the American character. It is the American character that protects our liberty and our freedoms. Democracy—sound democracy and the republic, its rule by law and reliance on principles that do not change—is not a cause but an effect of our national character, character in the leaders of our institutions, both economic and social, and character in our people. Our character is defined by the statement "In God We Trust." This we must never forget, that America is a secular nation in its political foundation, nation in a time when the union was in danger of dissolution. The American revolution and George Washington taught the world to know us. Abraham Lincoln and the Civil War taught us to know ourselves. The ideals of liberty, equality, and democracy are not just words on a piece of paper, but words to live by and stand straight to defend.

Woodrow Wilson saw his role in foreign policy as breaking away from the historic American policy of recognizing all governments in power. President Wilson was an active evangelist, preaching the chivalrous globalism of the American ideals. He wanted America to stay involved with the global community. The vision of the Wilsonian foreign policy was to refuse recognition of any government whose moral course and internal constitution was not acceptable to moral scrutiny. This moralistic approach was a departure from the historic policy that had been to recognize all governments in power. While being the ideal, foreign policy based on calculations or balance of power and national interest, the reliance on moral diplomacy was rife with pitfalls. It throws upon the United States the dubious responsibility of deciding which foreign governments were pure and which were not. When immoral foreign regimes survive, you lose prestige unless you can enforce your stance. The unpalatable alternatives are the possibility of having to retreat from its policy of non-recognition or to intervene actively to defend that policy, risking the possibility of war. Wilson saw entry into World War I as the right thing to do, as a moral choice in the face of a breakdown of civilization.

The Great War was entered into with the Wilsonian vision of America as fighting for her principles, not only for her interests. The Wilsonian vision of America's international role was messianic: America had to break away from a European diplomacy based on the balance of power. President Wilson was an active, chivalrous knight, a Galahad sitting in the "Seige Perilous" and that by him the holy grail should be achieved. Wilson believed in that "beacon on the summit of the mountain." He believed that the American character demanded that we recognize the fact that with the equal rights given to us by our Creator and spelled out in the Declaration of Independence we have equal responsibilities; namely, to share the word of the American gospel of *liberty, equality, and democracy.* The passage below was stated earlier in the definition of the American character, but it needs to be restated and affirmed again at this point in the process.

The Puritans brought with them the "Dream of Religious Freedom" and the unique American ideal of *liberty, equality, and democracy,* defined in the Declaration of Independence as *life,* some of the finest universities and colleges in the Western Hemisphere. They continue their destructive attacks on capitalism believing that the collapse of communism was the fault of those who attempted its reform. Many or most of them never seem to confront the moral issue posed by their destructive agendas.

"The explicit agenda of critical theory is to undermine the credibility and authority of the status quo in order to prepare its annihilation." Critical theory is the coy self-description of the ideological Left. It defines itself by the totality of its rejection of the existing social order.

Earl Warren, over the course of his life, came to value freedom more highly and to see security not as undermined by freedom but rather as its product. Must liberty be curtailed in order to preserve the nation, or is the nation better understood as an expression of its freedoms? No, it is better understood as an expression of its character, the American character. And if the American character is diminished or forsaken, then so are our freedoms. Liberty then becomes only a memory. The Warren Court never understood this, and I am not convinced that some of the current justices could ever understand this line of thought either.

Liberty and the pursuit of happiness are unalienable rights endowed by their Creator. It is the very heart and soul of what America was to become. It was the emergence of the *national character*, our *American character*.

Judicial activism as a form of moral relativism

Woodrow Wilson, with his liberal progressive agenda, pioneered the doctrine of a *living constitution* that today's liberals and as far back as Wilson and the New Deal of Franklin Roosevelt were using as the basis for their transformation of American politics. Wilson believed that the individual had no meaning apart from the society in which his individuality had been formed. Wilson and those progressives who followed him later on believed that freedom did not come from nature or from God, but is instead a product of the state and is realized only in the modern state. By removing the absolutes, liberalism has led to a reversal of human norms and natural law while, without knowing and with indifference, we have fallen into a wilderness of *moral relativism* and *moral equivalency*.

Diversity and moral relativism, where no idea is superior to another, are dangerous metaphors for division, confusion, and mediocrity. College students fall prey to what G. K. Chesterton said about the world of atheism, "When people stop believing in God, they don't believe in nothing, they believe in anything."

Following the communist collapse, the great majority of the secular progressive intellectuals continued their war against the democracies of the West and are now professors teaching in some of the finest universities and colleges in the Western Hemisphere. They continue their destructive attacks on capitalism believing that the collapse of communism was the fault of those who attempted its reform. Many or most of them never seem to confront the moral issues posed by their destructive agendas.

"The explicit agenda of critical theory is to undermine the credibility and authority of the status quo in order to prepare its annihilation." Critical theory is the coy self-description of the ideological Left. It defines itself by the totality of its rejection of the existing social order.

Earl Warren, over the course of his life, came to value freedom more highly and to see security not as undermined by freedom but rather as its product. Must liberty be curtailed in order to preserve the nation, or is the nation better understood as an expression of its character, which is defined in the Declarationof Independence as life, liberty, and the pursuit of happiness?

CHAPTER 10

―――― ⌒♁⌒ ――――

The Child and the World

The Weakness of Our Educational System

The first amendment states that "Congress shall make no law respecting an establishment of religion, or prohibiting the free exercise thereof."

The ACLU and the judiciary prefer to interpret Christianity as an establishment of religion rather than faith in a higher being that the founders of this nation trusted for guidance while defining this nation, its Christian heritage, and its constitution. Then to ignore the next sentence in the Bill of Rights which states that Congress shall make no law prohibiting the free exercise thereof.

Perhaps we should change the wording of the constitution to say that Congress and federal judges shall make no law prohibiting the free exercise thereof.

From these early days of the ratification of the constitution in 1789 until the court case of *Everson v. Board of Education* in 1947, the country had been spared "a misleading metaphor" as Justice William Rehnquist has described the "separation of church and state" expressed by President Thomas Jefferson in an exchange of letters with the Danbury Baptist Association. The court chose to take one sentence out of this exchange of letters and pass it off as the enforcement of a long-standing constitutional principle. Taken as a whole, the letters reflect Jefferson's true intent which is the same as the other founders. He believed that the first amendment had been enacted only to prevent the federal establishment of a national denomination. We are a Christian nation, and Congress has made no law respecting an establishment of religion or prohibiting the free exercise thereof.

The Supreme Court does not have the right to inject themselves into an area where there is no lawful basis for the courts or any element of the federal government to act. We are "one nation under God" and we shall remain that way, but we must fight against those who would take away the right to acknowledge God in our everyday lives.

Recently the Ninth Circuit Court of Appeals informed us that parents have no fundamental right as a parent to control the upbringing of their children in accordance with their personal and religious values and beliefs and no constitutional right to prevent the public schools from providing information on *whatever* in any form or manner they select.

Joshua Herring, in his article "Who Will Save the Children?" asks the question, "Where are they going with all this?" Well, it isn't toward the individualism that Christianity teaches. "The Christian idea of vocation, that unique role that each Christian plays in the cosmic drama of creation and redemption, is the one root of the Western idea of individualism. It was not, in its origins, a matter of self-constituting autonomy but of living out the singular, God-given destiny that is every human life."

The new education of today rests on two intellectual pillars: its use or misuse of science and its appeal to the educational philosophy of John Dewey and Charles Darwin.

The objectives of Dewey's educational theory and his general philosophy was that of the development of an educational theory that would be wholly consistent with Darwinism and the Origin of Species. In this sense, Dewey saw education as a major force in social reconstruction.

Perhaps an even better question might be "What manner of child shall this be?" Dewey believed that if society is to be remade, the child is placed at the center of the school and the rigid authority of the teacher and the traditional weight of the curriculum are displaced by his or her own developing interests and impulses. The role of the teacher becomes that of director of indoctrination and facilitator of the learning process that forms a type of character and mind suitable to the work of social reform. Pre-Darwinian theory had no trace of the more sophisticated functionalist psychology of Dewey's writings.

Most of the early writings of John Steinbeck are filled with near biblical Old Testament expressions of a fundamental theme, that theme of the need for a moral choice as an identifying mark of the human condition—a choice between good and evil. Today we are faced with that same choice to keep out of nature's way and not to corrupt that childhood as it comes fresh from the hands of God or allow a malevolent system of morals and philosophy to shatter irretrievably all that Christianity has rendered possible.

Progressive education is socialism in its most malevolent and destructive form. It is evil and it will destroy Christianity and democracy as it tears away at the very fabric of our constitution, which is based upon Christian principles.

Coming back to the original issue, in the 1950s, conservative Christianity was vilified as being anti-intellectual. The socialist philosophy of John Dewey and his theories of education as a means of social reconstruction are pervasive and are taught in every school of education in every university in this country. Teachers no longer are required to know their subject; they must, however, be well trained in the methods of teaching socialist indoctrination.

Dewey always feared that the teacher, as the responsible adult, was the prime source of conformity. Instead of having finally produced a program to liberate the child from unimpeded growth, as American educators still believe, placing the child squarely at the center, defining education as growth without end, and so weighing the discussion of educational goals, and a quarter of a century of explanation and clarification statements, were not enough for Dewey to hold in check the anti-intellectual perversions of his theory.

Short of open rebellion, civil war, and revolution, how do we fight back when the opponents are so well entrenched? There is no question that as Christians, there will be sacrifice and determination is the order of the day.

The ACLU and the National Education Association are well funded and have been promoting socialistic ideology since the 1920s. Congress was unable to get a bill though that would have cut off funds to the ACLU, the Public Expression of Religion Act; and while the liberal Left is always willing to burn books to advance science, they refuse the mention of IQ in any context.

It is obvious then that the goal of the liberal Left is not to educate our children, but to indoctrinate our offspring in the doctrines of what Ann Coulter calls the "church of liberalism." It is the same method used by Islam in their religious schools of indoctrination.

There are positive steps that can be taken, but the road is long and hard. We have two choices. Basically, we can ignore the present educational system and start a Christian system which provides pride in the possession of intellect and joy, as a child of God made in His image, in the use of that intellect. Or we can attempt to tear down what is already in place. The former makes more sense. But we must do it and not just talk about it.

Step 1: Change the manner in which our children are educated by stopping the broad assault on religious liberty and family autonomy. The list of academic institutions that preaches and teaches anti-American and anti-Christian dogma to our children is growing daily. Perhaps by expanding Christian education or promoting the complete revamping of our teacher education programs at the university level and by closing all schools of education and requiring teachers to know their subject by attaining a degree in that subject. Bill Bennett and David Horowitz know how difficult this would be.

There is much to be said for a *classical education* in the form of the traditional seven liberal arts embodied in the disciplines of the *trivium* and the *quadrivium*. Progressive education advocates will immediately pronounce this as turning the wheel back toward the Middle Ages. The truth is that presently our children are taught more courses, but they know less. This simply means that while we cram more and more facts into our children's brain, they are being deprived of the tools of learning. Information overload deprives them of the ability to think objectively; they learn everything, but the art of learning and the tools of learning are the same in any and every subject.

The objectives of Dewey's educational theory and his general philosophy was that of the development of an educational theory that would be wholly consistent with Darwinism and the Origin of Species. In this sense, Dewey saw education as a major force in social reconstruction.

Step 2: Promote a renewal of political movement such as that stated in Pope Leo XIII's encyclical Rerum Novarum of 1891. The need to include both Catholic and Protestant strains of Christian democracy is obvious. The secularism of the European Union seems to have stopped the movement from flowering in France and Germany as well as other countries of the union. However, it is showing strength in unexpected places such as Eastern Bloc nations like Poland and Rumania.

There is a legacy left from Europe's experiment in Christian democracy which might provide lessons for us all.

First, the movement has had the most success when it has held true to the *full* gospel, particularly to Christ's radical command that we love our neighbors as ourselves. Issues of social welfare and social justice lie near the heart of true Christian democracy.

Second, this movement successfully pioneered ways to funnel public health, education, and welfare programs through churches and church-related agencies, models that should be of interest to a nation now experimenting with faith-based initiatives.

Third, Christian democracy has, at its best, carved out a *third way* of social-economic policy, independent of both the liberal-capitalist and socialist mind-sets, by being respectful toward family life and the health of local communities.

And fourth, this movement succeeded only so long as it found animation in authentic Christian faith and enthusiasm. When those diminished, so did the coherence and effectiveness of Christian democracy and of the European nations as a whole. I do not know if it is the answer to the current republican failure to hold to the conservative principles of Ronald Reagan, but they might get the idea that true conservatives are serious.

Christians are always fighting from a defensive position. The ACLU and their atheist plaintiffs sue every time they can find a cross or the Ten Commandments vulnerable to their blackmail. Why not go on the offense and treat liberalism as a religion?

Here are some excerpts from a link called the *Education Reporter*. This report also contains the quote from the Harvard professor, Chester M. Pierce. After reading this you will realize how long and why they have been engaged in taking over our educational system. As I stated in an earlier post, Christianity teaches children mutual respect for the individual and each other and how to think for themselves. It will take more than a maximum effort to stop these people in their quest for socialism.

> Every child in America entering school at the age of five is mentally ill because he comes to school with certain allegiances to our Founding Fathers, toward our elected officials, toward his parents, toward a belief in a supernatural being, and toward the sovereignty of this nation as a separate entity. It's up to you as teachers to make all these sick children well—by creating the international child of the future.

Norman Thomas, a socialist and member of the American Civil Liberties Union, boldly told the world, "The American people will never knowingly adopt socialism, but under the name of liberalism, they will adopt every fragment of the socialist program until one day America will be a socialist nation without ever knowing how it happened."

John Dewey, known as "the father of modern education," was an avowed socialist and the coauthor of the *Humanist Manifesto*. The U.S. House Committee on Un-American Activities discovered that he belonged to fifteen Marxist-front organizations. Dewey taught the professors who trained America's teachers. Obsessed with *the group*, he said, "You can't make socialists out of individualists. Children who know how to think for themselves spoil the harmony of the collective society, which is coming, where everyone is interdependent."

Was Abraham Lincoln, and were many of our founders, *done a disservice* by being homeschooled? No doubt if they had undergone Dewey's utopia of government education, they could have made something of themselves!

Indeed they and our nation would have been done a disservice had they been subjected to the anti-intellectual perversions of his theory.

CHAPTER 11

The ACLU and Judicial Supremacy

The wolf is at the door again. The ACLU is still trying to convince us that they, and only they, are the defenders of our civil rights. The ACLU is the product of a malevolent system of warped morals and antihuman philosophy. They are the snake in the garden of Eden holding out the apple as a seductive illusion of power granted to those who are foolish enough to believe their "enlightened" thinking.

The ACLU is a product of Enlightenment conspirators who had produced a system of morals and philosophy which is, in the words of Winston Churchill, "as malevolent as Christianity was benevolent, which, if not arrested would shatter irretrievably all that Christianity has rendered possible." This malignant worldview "has been the mainspring of every subversive movement during the nineteenth century. This worldwide conspiracy for the overthrow of civilization and the reconstitution of society on the basis of arrested development, of envious malevolence, and impossible equality has been steadily growing" (Zionism versus Bolshevism).

The ACLU and their theology of secular humanism (communism in disguise) is attempting to gain power through the reversal of human norms, natural law, and the social institutions that are so necessary for the continuance of mankind and our republican form of government.

In his book *The Everlasting Man*, G. K. Chesterton described this reversal process as the *theology of demons* and said that it was sadistically antihuman and anti-childhood. It is intrinsically evil. It is a malignancy-filled system of philosophy posturing as something seemingly innocuous in order to infect Christendom and Christianity in the United States.

The ACLU is a major carrier of this infectious disease as they mount attacks on each and every aspect of religious and individual expression in our daily lives. They seek to enslave not to defend our freedoms.

Social justice agendas were launched in the name of civil rights and other rights that exist only in the minds of nine justices of the Supreme Court who were never elected to any legislative office and with the sole purpose of creating in America a cultural revolution in which God no longer dominates the moral horizon and personal autonomy and individual choice become the twin pillars of a debased moral view. Those who believe in an active judiciary have designated the Supreme Court as an elitist tool for passing legislation that otherwise cannot pass in Congress because it violates the true will of the people.

The attack on the constitution may or may not have started with Roe v. Wade, but it certainly was a critical juncture that opened up for Justice Harry Blackmun and his view that the document he had sworn to uphold could and should be altered according to liberal prejudice and judicial whim rather than the republic's rule by law and the founders' idea of principles that do not change.

The march toward judicial supremacy has a long and storied history and has been sharply contested. Constitutional law classes always begin with *Marbury v. Madison (1803) as the confirmation of the Supreme Court's supremacy*. Others claim that its roots can be traced to the American founding era, that the written constitution implies no less. Nothing is further from the truth. Judicial supremacy is in fact a thoroughly modern development having been invented by the Supreme Court itself and asserted for the first time in *Cooper v. Aaron*, the 1958 Little Rock school's case. The patience of the Court's justices had been exhausted by the opposition to *Brown v. Board of Education* (1954). They, therefore, decreed that its decisions were "supreme in the exposition of the law of the constitution." The court, for the first time, declared in the *Cooper opinion* that the supremacy clause effectively equated the authority of the federal judicial opinions with that of the constitution's text.

Johnathan O'Neill, in his splendid investigation of the issue of judicial review, suggests there is more to the story and argues that it is "rooted in the revolt against formalism," a movement inspired, in more or less equal parts, by philosophical pragmatism, legal positivism, Darwinian theory, and progressive reformism.

Abraham Lincoln stated, "If the policy of the Government upon vital questions affecting the whole people is to be irrevocably fixed by decisions of the Supreme Court...the people will have ceased to be their own rulers, having to that extent practically resigned their Government into the hands of that eminent tribunal."

Woodrow Wilson stated that when the public recognized that the spirit of the constitution has been violated, the public would make "such outrages upon constitutional morality impossible by standing ready to curse them." I think it is now time to stand ready and curse them. Justices Kennedy, Stevens, who retired and has been replaced by Eleana Kagan, Breyer, Souter, who has since been replaced by Sonia Sotomajor and Ginsberg are worthy of the contempt of the American people. They should be tarred and feathered for their treasonous acts.

It is time to take a stand and make it known, remembering the words of Abraham Lincoln, that the people will not cease to be their own rulers. That the Supreme Court does not have the right to irrevocably fix decisions upon vital questions affecting the whole people. I will not surrender, I will not surrender the constitution, I will not surrender my individual will, and I will not surrender my government into the hands of that *eminent* tribunal. Thomas Jefferson felt that the aim of self-government is not the satisfaction of desires, but the incarnation of our free will. This is the true meaning of freedom.

The Bill of Rights mean nothing to the American people unless they are strengthened and maintained by the constitutional principle of checks and balances and the separation of powers between the three branches of government: the executive branch, the legislative branch, and the judicial branch. They are meant to balance out in order to prevent any one branch from attaining supremacy.

However, since the 1920s, with the help of people like the ACLU, the balance has shifted to an elitist court that sees the constitution as a *living organism* that can be changed or interpreted to say whatever they want it to say.

This is the real danger of the ACLU. Their aim is to destroy the Bill of Rights along with the constitution of the United States. The ACLU is intrinsically evil. It is the definitive evil.

"Ayn Rand has shown that the evil is the irrational, willful denial and evasion of the facts of reality. It is the deliberate defiance of the facts and laws of nature, a spitting in the face of existence. Human survival requires rationality, a commitment to discover and act on the full truth. Evil men stand opposed to this—to reality, to the rational, to every value on which human life depends."

Because of this, evil is metaphysically impotent: it cannot build, grow, create, or produce. Achievements require commitment to the laws and facts of reality. As stated by Francis Bacon, "Nature, to be commanded, must be obeyed." Men who forsake nature, whether to follow their own whims, conform to the group, or obey God, are incapable of producing or prospering on their own. Criminals, dictators, tribal warlords, Washington bureaucrats, and welfare leeches create and achieve nothing. Left to their own devices, they would huddle in caves and die. The irrational is helpless, utterly powerless."

There are many little known facts about the ACLU of which most people are not aware. There is a little known 1976 federal law called the Civil Rights Attorney's Fees Awards Act which allows the ACLU to collect attorney's fees for its suits against the Ten Commandments and all of the crosses it can find throughout this land. Kentucky taxpayers paid $121,500 to the ACLU for their action against the Ten Commandments displayed in two county courthouses. Tennessee paid $50,000 and Alabama paid $540,000. The ACLU profited more than $160,000 in court costs from their suit against the Boy Scouts of America. This is not a list of good works.

The very fact that the Founding Fathers' belief in a supreme being and the constitution that they gave to us is based on Christian tradition, and values is the very reason that all other religions are protected. The ACLU has an agenda, and it has nothing to do with civil rights. They are using the courts and the judicial activism of the courts to write law by fiat. Its agenda is to destroy the very source and foundation of the American character and replace it with atheistic humanism. Several court cases filed by the ACLU and Americans United for Separation of Church and State against the school districts in Cobb County, Georgia and Dover, Pennsylvania has resulted in decisions that allowed Darwinists to remain supreme in the secular sanctity of the public schools.

Congress, as the elected representatives of the people, must reclaim their role in the balance of power struggle with the judicial branch. The wisdom of the Founding Fathers was most evident when they created the separation of powers with the three branches of government. The constitution defines the specific powers of each branch. No one branch is greater than the other two, and Congress must act soon to bring balance to the system once again. The republic, its rule by law and reliance on principles that do not change, is not a cause but an effect of our national character. The ACLU's agenda is to destroy our national character and in turn destroy our biblical republic and our reliance on God as our Creator and the self-evident truths defined by the Declaration of Independence.

Norman Thomas, a socialist and member of the American Civil Liberties Union, boldly told the world, "The American people will never knowingly adopt socialism, but under the name of liberalism, they will adopt every fragment of the socialist program until one day America will be a socialist nation without ever knowing how it happened."

John Dewey, known as "the father of modern education," was an avowed socialist and the coauthor of the *Humanist Manifesto*. The U.S. House Committee on Un-American Activities discovered that he belonged to fifteen Marxist-front organizations. Dewey taught the professors who trained America's teachers. Obsessed with *the group*, he said, "You can't make socialists out of individualists. Children who know how to think for themselves spoil the harmony of the collective society, which is coming, where everyone is interdependent."

Roger Nash Baldwin, who was an avowed socialist and defender of Communist Russia, was the guiding force for the ACLU for many years until his death in 1981 at the age of ninety-seven.

Baldwin was born into a world of wealth and privilege and grew up in an area of Massachusetts representative of the comfort and affluence of an old-stock New England family. Harvard-educated, Baldwin first gained national prominence as a social worker in St. Louis, befriended by Jane Addams, well-known social worker and antiwar activist of Chicago and Hull House fame. This was the progressive era of the early twentieth century. With the Wilson administration and United States involvement in World War I, Baldwin and socialist Norman Thomas began promoting such organizations as the American Union Against Militarism and the National Civil Liberties Bureau.

Baldwin was convinced that anarchism was intellectually respectable. Baldwin had developed a life-long pattern of involvement with both reformist and radical circles. He wanted to be respectable and associate with anarchists at the same time and so developed an early affinity for the rebel, the heretic, the radical. Baldwin himself referred to this as "the dualism in my life—conformity and radicalism...in the Boston pattern...I consciously identified myself with these people...gentlemen radicals, aristocratic radicals" like Thoreau. As a teenager, Baldwin attended a lecture by John Fiske, author of *The Nature of God*. Fiske was the American philosopher who did much to popularize the theory of evolution.

The ACLU is an example and a product of the dualism of Baldwin's personality. It is interesting that Baldwin began his public career as a social worker and then later became a social reformer. In the mind of the social reformer there is a Marxist philosophy inherent in their thinking. It is that the human essence is no abstraction inherent in each single individual. In its reality it is the ensemble of the social relations. It also follows from this belief that if you can change the ensemble of the social relations, you can totally change human nature. The value of the individual as taught by Christianity is not important to the ACLU. Only the disappearance of individual freedoms that the dual face of the ACLU promotes through collective, liberal, and fanatical views that will lead this nation toward tyranny.

In attempting to understand the basic differences between all the atheist movements that have in the past and even in the present, through varying philosophies, attempted to change human nature, they have all failed except one. Christianity teaches the value of the individual while Darwinism, communism, and all of the other isms try to change human nature through a collective system of political and economic thought and control. "It was the scientific method as applied to all facets of life, more than any particular scientific theory, that lay at the heart of modernity—but Darwinism was critical in applying that method to the key issues of biological origins and human morality" (Larson 1997). In viewing the battle between atheism and Christianity, I continue to fall back on the wisdom of Charles Schultz as he described his famous cartoon character, Charlie Brown. He always said that Charlie Brown was an inner-directed person living in an outer-directed world. Christianity wants to change the individual from the inside.

The ACLU has become very selective about what it considers *free* speech. They pick and choose the cases and the locations in order to gain advantage with judges, courts, and state legislatures. This method was behind the Scopes "Monkey" Trial in Dayton, Tennessee, in 1925. The ACLU had a preconceived idea of how to attack fundamentalism, and the state of Tennessee provided the perfect opportunity for them to apply that idea when the introduction of a bill in the legislature made it a felony to teach evolution in the public schools of the state. The anti-evolutionists had been busy in the state since the 1923 legislature failed to pass any bills to outlaw the teaching of evolution. They began targeting Tennessee and North Carolina as states most likely to pass legislation more to their liking. Unwittingly their efforts provided the perfect venue for the ACLU and their desire to attack and condemn "the monstrous nonsense of fundamentalism."

The antievolution crusade did not cause the chasm or create the cleavage; it simply exposed it. Generations of Americans prior to this era of the 1920s, especially those of Protestant European roots, tended to share a common system of values. It was the rise of positivism and Darwinism that changed the field of analysis of how and what we believe. By the early twentieth century a widening gap was detected between the God-fearing American majority and the disbelieving cultural elite.

William Jennings Bryan, in a script that cast him as the defender of Christianity, was pitted against Clarence Darrow, the atheist. It was a courtroom drama straight from a Broadway play written and directed by the ACLU for the sole purpose of pitting science and religion in a battle to determine their place in public education. The fact is it became a Broadway play.

Inherit the Wind is running on Broadway again, with the righteously rational atheist attorney Clarence Darrow fighting on the side of reason and science against the Bible-thumping champion of the antievolutionist movement William Jennings Bryan. The play and the subsequent movie portrayed a level of intolerance and implied that antievolution laws left only biblical creationism alone as being taught in the classroom. The play, as written, was a complete fabrication meant to capture the precise moment in American history when science and reason destroyed for all time the superstition and the myth of those foolish reactionaries who believe in God and the Bible.

From the case of *Everson v. Board of Education*, 330 US 1 1947, the Supreme Court and its ACLU allies have provided a steady stream of court decisions that contradict the clear, literal, and intended meaning of the constitution. The *Everson* decision was the first mention of "a wall of separation between church and state." That misleading metaphor was first mentioned by then President Thomas Jefferson in a letter to the Baptist Association of Danbury, Connecticut. There is no mention of a wall of separation in the constitution. Mr. Justice Black used the metaphor in writing the majority opinion for the court. It was nothing more than a vague reference. "New Jersey has not in the slightest breached a wall between church and state. Its statute is therefore constitutional." In this case the court ruled against the plaintiff five to four and in favor of the New Jersey statute that allowed boards of education to reimburse parents, including those whose children went to Catholic parochial schools, for the cost of bus transportation to and from school.

Other decisions include:

1) banning nondenominational prayer from public schools *(Engel v. Vitale, 370 US 42 1, 435n.21 1962)*;

2) banning Bible reading from public schools except for comparative religion and history study *(Abington Township v. Schempp 374 US 203, 304 1963)*, striking down a state's choice not to teach the evolution of humans (Epperson v. Arkansas, 393 US 97 1968);

3) removing the Ten Commandments from public school walls, (Stone v. Graham, 449 US 39 1980);

4) striking down "a period of silence not to exceed one minute...for meditation or voluntary prayer" (Wallace v. Jaffree, 472 US 38 101–102 1985);

5) censoring creationist viewpoints when evolutionist viewpoints are taught (Edwards v. Aguillard, 482 US 578 1987); and

6) barring prayers at public school graduations (Lee v. Weisman, 112 S. Ct. 2678, 2683–84 1992).

This is Scopes II, a continuation of the Scopes Monkey Trial, where all the nonsense started in Tennessee in 1925. The Arkansas Supreme Court reversed the trial judges' ruling in the Epperson case. A young biology instructor named Susan Epperson served as the nominal plaintiff for the ACLU and their role in overturning the antievolution statutes of the state of Arkansas. These statutes had been the result of a popular referendum adopted by Arkansas voters in the wake of the Scopes Trial but were never enforced.

The right to privacy is one of those phony constitutional rights that liberals cannot run on openly because it sounds very similar to the ideological agenda of the ACLU. Instead they rely on the courts to ensure the right of a minor girl to have a partial birth abortion without parental notification.

Justice Antonin Scalia has spoken out on this phenomenon of the gains of the homosexual lobby over the past few decades. They are another group that liberalism has placed beneath their protective umbrella of oppressed minorities. In the case of Bowers v. Hardwick (1986), the U.S. Supreme Court could find nothing in the constitution that gave anyone or guaranteed anyone the right to engage in homosexual sodomy. Suddenly, some fifteen to twenty years later in *Romer v. Evans (1996)*, the Supreme Court struck down a Colorado amendment to the state constitution that had been adopted by the voters of Colorado in a referendum that prohibited the state government or any counties or cities within the state from giving homosexuals, as a class, special protection.

In Justice Scalia's view, the court's holding in Bowers protected the right of states to pass laws that disfavor homosexuality. The amendment at issue in *Romer* simply denied them from receiving special treatment under Colorado law. Scalia further wrote that the court's opinion in contradicting *Bowers* "places the prestige of this institution behind the proposition that opposition to homosexuality is as reprehensible as racial or religious bias."

Later, in *Lawrence v. Texas (2003)*, the Supreme Court, while not declaring homosexual sodomy as legal, they liberated themselves from the text of the constitution, from the text, and even from the traditions of the American people of the last 200 years. The court suddenly found that there was no text in the constitution that you could reinterpret to create a right to anything, such as homosexual sodomy or abortion. They needed something else, and that something else is called the doctrine of *substantive due process*. The constitution has a due process clause, which states that no person shall be deprived of life, liberty, or property without due process of law. It is a guarantee that the law cannot prosecute, fine, incarcerate, or execute you without following the procedural guarantee defined by due process. The Supreme Court, going back as far as the Dred Scott case, has said that there are some liberties that are so important that no process will suffice or is capable of taking them away. So, therefore, we have the right to privacy as one liberty defined by substantive due process. The doctrine of substantive due process was initially to embrace only those liberties that are fundamental to a democratic society and rooted in the traditions of the American people. In the last twenty years or so, that limitation has been totally eliminated and judicially manufactured notions have arbitrarily established the constitutional right to alter the moral framework of our nation.

The senator from Massachusetts, the late Edward Kennedy and his friends from the liberal Left, have argued for more activist judges on both the Supreme Court and the federal courts. Kennedy argues that this is the only way his socially liberal policies can be enacted, not by the usual method of legislation passed in Congress through the republican process of representative democracy, but by judicial fiat. Kennedy prefers this method rather than trust the American public. Liberals, by and large, do not believe in the American character and the individualism taught by Christianity. That is why liberalism is the most dangerous enemy that we, as a Christian nation, face today.

Inherit the Wind and Evolution
The Scopes Trial and the ACLU

The Scopes Trial and the fact that it was a plot and a timeline scripted by the ACLU clearly shows that their goal then was the same as it is today: to promote secular or atheistic humanism through the reversal of human norms.

Norman Thomas, a socialist and member of the American Civil Liberties Union, boldly told the world, "The American people will never knowingly adopt socialism, but under the name of liberalism, they will adopt every fragment of the socialist program until one day America will be a socialist nation without ever knowing how it happened."

John Dewey, known as "the father of modern education," was an avowed socialist and the coauthor of the *Humanist Manifesto*. The U.S. House Committee on Un-American Activities discovered that he belonged to fifteen Marxist-front organizations. Dewey taught the professors who trained America's teachers.

Obsessed with *the group*, he said, "You can't make socialists out of individualists. Children who know how to think for themselves spoil the harmony of the collective society, which is coming, where everyone is interdependent."

The main points that were made are spelled out in these two sentences: "What was at stake for the communities in Tennessee was whether it was good that schoolchildren be taught that they descended from apes, rather than being made in God's image." "And that was what the Tennessee lawmakers objected to: the promotion of Darwin's ideas as moral guidance."

The new education of today rests on two intellectual pillars: its use or misuse of science and its appeal to the educational philosophy of John Dewey.

The objectives of Dewey's educational theory and his general philosophy was that of the development of an educational theory that would be wholly consistent with Darwinism and the Origin of Species. In this sense, Dewey saw education as a major force in social reconstruction.

Perhaps an even better question might be "What manner of child shall this be?" Dewey believed that if society is to be remade, the child is placed at the center of the school and the rigid authority of the teacher and the traditional weight of the curriculum are displaced by his or her own developing interests and impulses. The role of the teacher becomes that of director of indoctrination and facilitator of the learning process that forms a type of character and mind suitable to the work of social reform. Pre-Darwinian theory had no trace of the more sophisticated functionalist psychology of Dewey's writings.

William Jennings Bryan warned in one of his books that "Nietzsche carried Darwinism to its logical conclusion and denied the existence of God, denounced Christianity as the doctrine of the degenerate, and democracy as the refuge of the weakling; he overthrew all standards of morality and eulogized war as necessary to man's development." The 1916 survey of religious belief among college students and professors published by the Bryn Mawr University psychologist James H. Leuba confirmed Bryan's worst fears. Leuba concluded that Christianity, as a system of belief, has utterly broken down and it was becoming practically a national epidemic. It has become progressively worse as time goes by. The number of negative posts that you received in response to your article is telling. You have to question what some of these people are reading, or if they read at all.

The movie *Inherit the Wind* is a total misrepresentation of the facts of the Scopes Trial and shows the extent to which Hollywood is willing to go in promoting their own agenda. Americans must stay informed in the matters that influence us as well as our children.

The fake vertebrate embryo exhibit created by one of Darwin's most ardent supporters led Darwin himself to believe the lie and proclaim that it was by far the strongest single class of facts in favor of his theory. The German scientist Ernst Haeckel had coined the slogan "Ontogeny recapitulates phylogeny," which means each individual embryo replays all the prior stages of evolution. More than a hundred years ago, in Haeckel's own day, scientists already knew that he had faked the sketches, but the scientific community has only now begun to expose this falsehood. Haeckel's principle of recapitulation, that the human embryo replays the steps of evolution, has also been proven false, but it lives on in arguments used to justify abortion and stem cell research. After all, according to this discredited science, we start out as something less than human while the transformation takes place gradually.

Clarence Darrow was not content with simply questioning popular notions of criminal responsibility, but he delighted in challenging traditional concepts of religion and morality. One historian described Darrow as "the last of the 'village atheists' on a national scale." He regarded Christianity as a *slave religion*, encouraging acquiescence in injustice, a willingness to make do with the mediocre, and complacency in the face of the intolerable. He called himself an agnostic, but in fact he was effectively an atheist. Darrow often invoked the idea of organic evolution to support his arguments, but it was never central to his thinking. He claimed to understand modern biology but mixed up Darwinian, Lamarckian, and mutation-theory concepts in his arguments, utilizing whichever best served his immediate rhetorical purposes. He frequently appealed to science as an objective arbitrator of truth but would only present scientific evidence that supported his position. The fact is Darrow was a lawyer, and as such he would go the direction needed to win his case.

The reason that I left Bill Clinton out of the previous writings about the lies of John Kerry and Lyndon B. Johnson was simply because of the parallel of the war stories related and amplified by the two were so similar in their apparent need to further ambitions and the inner needs of the two were almost identical. Clinton raises the lie to a new art form. His inner need to lie may be similar to Kerry and Johnson in the furthering of ambitions, but I think psychologically the origin may be more related to childhood and absence of values in the home and the codependency of the family. It is becoming more and more apparent that the media is willing to accept the lie and ignore its effect on society and the country if you confess the transgression after the fact and ask for forgiveness with a tear in your eye. Then it becomes society who is to blame.

Just recently I heard an interview of a woman married to a gay man. She said that she blamed society for the pressure society placed on her husband to marry rather than face life as a gay. Whatever happened to doing the right thing in the first place! Now we have the coming out of the governor of New Jersey, Jim McGreevey, who, by all indications, is the totally corrupt leader of a state that is totally corrupt with Democratic Party control. The Democratic Party grip on this state is such that the people of New Jersey are powerless to do anything about the mess. "My truth is that I am a gay American." This may be the truth, just not the whole truth. I tend to believe that McGreevey is probably bisexual, but to admit this and use this as a reason to resign would not evoke the sympathetic response that "I am a gay American" does. This is probably nothing more than a political move to elicit compassion and cover his criminal actions as governor of the state of New Jersey. Just as Bill Clinton stated that he did not have sexual relations with that woman, Ms. Lewinsky. Was that the truth, the whole truth, nothing but the truth, so help you, God? Since the liberal democrats and the ACLU insist on no mention of God in anything, I suppose we are left with no way of getting anyone to take an oath to tell the truth, the whole truth and nothing but the truth, so help you, God. Truth is whatever these politicians and the liberal press can get the American public to believe. As Hillary Clinton would say, "It takes a village," a village of idiots.

CHAPTER 12

---❦---

On the Separation of Church and State

Since the end of World War II, our institutions and our national character have come under ever-increasing attack from those who then claim protection under the first amendment of the constitution. I do not wish to deny them this right nor to deny the principle of free speech. I do wish, however, to stop the erosion of the rights of the many by the working agenda of the few.

The first amendment states that "Congress shall make no law respecting an establishment of religion, or prohibiting the free exercise thereof."

For too long now we have seen the courts uphold the rights of a lone dissenter only to take away the rights of the many. The ACLU and the judiciary prefer to interpret Christianity as an establishment of religion rather than faith in a higher being that the founders of this nation trusted for guidance while defining this nation, its Christian heritage, and its constitution, only to ignore the next sentence in the Bill of Rights which states that Congress shall make no law prohibiting the free exercise thereof. Perhaps we should change the wording of the constitution to say that Congress and federal judges shall make no law prohibiting the free exercise thereof.

In this instance it would appear that Madison's thinking and his central aim to stop people from turning easily to the government for help is a lost exercise of the intellect. The judiciary branch of government, the federal judges who are not elected but appointed and therefore are not representatives of the people as such, have given to themselves a power that the constitution does not give even to Congress. The real issue then is whether or not any federal judge has the right to interfere with state actions that may or may not have anything to do with or constitute an establishment of religion. The tenth amendment to the constitution states that "The powers not delegated to the United States by the constitution, nor prohibited by it to the States, are reserved to the States respectively, or to the people." The power to make laws regarding an establishment of religion, having been explicitly withheld from the United States by the tenth amendment, is therefore reserved to the states or to the people.

The words of three of the early leaders and founders of this nation serve as a haunting reminder of the need to protect and cherish our Christian heritage and our national character.

A general dissolution of principles and manners will more surely overthrow the liberties of America than the whole force of the common enemy. While the people are virtuous they cannot be subdued; but when once they lose their virtue then will be ready to surrender their liberties to the first external or internal invader. (Adams 1779)

The Constitution which at any time exists, till changed by an explicit and authentic act of the whole People is sacredly obligatory upon all. (Washington 1796)

Statesmen, my dear Sir, may plan and speculate for Liberty, but it is Religion and Morality alone, which can establish the Principles upon which Freedom can securely stand...The only foundation of a free Constitution, is pure Virtue, and if this cannot be inspired into our People, in a great Measure, than they have it now, They

may change their Rulers, and the forms of
Government, but they will not obtain a lasting
Liberty. (Adams 1776)

From these early days of the ratification of the constitution in
1789 until the court case of *Everson v. Board of Education* in 1947,
the country had been spared *a misleading metaphor* as Justice William
Rehnquist has described the *separation of church and state* expressed
by President Thomas Jefferson in an exchange of letters with the
Danbury Baptist Association. The court chose to take one sentence
out of this exchange of letters and pass it off as the enforcement of a
long-standing constitutional principle. Taken as a whole, the letters
reflect Jefferson's true intent which is the same as the other founders. He believed that the first amendment had been enacted only to
prevent the federal establishment of a national denomination. We
are a Christian nation, and Congress has made no law respecting an
establishment of religion or prohibiting the free exercise thereof. The
Supreme Court does not have the right to inject themselves into an
area where there is no lawful basis for the courts or any element of
the federal government to act. We are "one nation under God" and
we shall remain that way, but we must fight against those who would
take away the right to acknowledge God in our everyday lives.

CHAPTER 13

―――――― ⌀ ――――――

The Origins of American Foreign Policy

With the presidency of Theodore Roosevelt and the emergence of the celebrated *bully pulpit*, the executive branch of government began to break from the traditions of the past and establish a dialogue and a direct relationship with the people. It was not, however, until Woodrow Wilson took office in 1913 that the rhetorical presidency was established and institutionalized.

Wilson argued that the president "has no [other] means of compelling Congress" and that the office should be used to sway public opinion. Wilson now saw the president as a national leader and spokesman, "the only national voice in affairs," who could be irresistible in dealing with Congress so long as he understood and led public opinion. Both Theodore Roosevelt and Woodrow Wilson were able to provide strong leadership because their techniques of leadership and their ability to assert the position of the president as the spokesman of the people and to use public opinion as a spur on Congress. The president must give voice to the highest aspirations of the American people first and then to the people of the world.

Prior to the Roosevelt and the Wilson administrations, the isolationist tendency prevailed in American foreign policy. The rapidly expanding American power and the gradual collapse of the international system centered on Europe were the two main factors that projected America into world affairs.

George F. Kennan, who in 1947 formulated the idea of containment which sought to contain the Soviet Union and its empire within its present reach, was Professor Emeritus in the School of Historical Studies at the Institute for Advanced Study in Princeton, New Jersey. At a dinner given in recognition of his ninetieth birthday, the author of these lines in an article written for *Foreign Affairs*, "On American Principles," ventured to say that what our country needed at this point was not primarily policies, much less a single policy. What we needed, he argued, were principles—sound principles, "principles that accorded with the nature, the needs, the interests, and the limitations of our country."

Faced with demands for support from rebellious Spanish colonies in South America following the Napoleonic Wars, Secretary of State John Quincy Adams enunciated a principle of American foreign policy that is still relevant today: the best way for a larger country to help smaller ones is by the power of example. To go further, Adams warned, would be "to involve America beyond the power of extrication in all the wars of interest and intrigue."

John Quincy Adams was the secretary of state during the presidency of James Monroe (1817–1825) when he realized that the United States historical experience left no choice but to welcome and give moral support to all peoples in their struggle for the recognition and consolidation of their independence. Adams was enunciating a principle of American foreign policy: namely, that while it was "the well-wisher to the freedom and independence of all," America was also "the champion and vindicator only of her own."

Oddly enough, herein lies a misunderstanding. America's current predicament has yielded up a yearning for what the editor of *Foreign Affairs* has called "the perennial hangover cure" for American foreign policy—realism. There is an unrealistic quality of realism to be found in this oft-quoted dictum, as it was expressed by the former career diplomat, which formed only a tiny part of a July 4 speech that Adams delivered in 1820. The rest of the speech is mostly ignored by Kennan, who was the author of the now-famous *Long Telegram* that outlined the dangers of Soviet expansion.

In his July 4 speech of 1820, Adams continued by saying that the Declaration of Independence was "the first solemn declaration by a nation of the only legitimate foundation of civil government. It was the cornerstone of a new fabric, destined to cover the surface of the globe. It stands, and must forever stand alone, a beacon on the summit of the mountain, to which all the inhabitants of the earth may turn their eyes for a genial and saving light till time shall be lost in eternity, and this globe itself dissolve, nor leave a wreck behind." Considering both statements, Adams is confronting realism with idealism.

President Ronald Reagan found several areas of disagreement with U.S. Cold War foreign policy. Reagan was consistent in the 1970s with his dislike of the Yalta conference and the resulting Soviet Empire's betrayal of Eastern Europe. He felt very strongly for the people of these nations and the brutality of the communist system. Reagan believed that the concepts of containment and detente did nothing to free these people from the chains of oppression and captivity. Ronald Reagan had a vision for and of America that the Soviet's Evil Empire must be faced and defeated. He flatly rejected the idea of containment.

Reagan had a vision for the restoration of America. Reagan wanted a confident America, one that would protect and promote freedom throughout the world, a global leader that would serve as a shining city upon a hill. Reagan was Wilsonian in his ideas of America being a light of liberty that would "shine unto the nations," acting not just as a model of liberty but a purveyor of the American character and its message of liberty, equality, and democracy. Both Wilson and Reagan, as well as Winthrop, felt that America has been blessed by a special providence that required the leadership of the United States of America. However, there are striking differences between the Wilson and Reagan administration in their vision for America. Wilson was a progressive who shared intellectual roots with European socialism and nationalism. The urgent needs and requirements of World War I allowed for the implementation of socialism on a war footing. The Wilson administration's philosophy was one of *essentialism* where the ultimate reality lies in the essence of things rather than in things themselves. Ronald Reagan believed that the problems we faced as a nation could not be solved by the government because government was the problem. He held on to faith in the individual and a moral imperative of the West to generate the collapse of communism. The morality dimension of Reagan was quite different from the hardline anti-communist *realpolitik* of Richard Nixon and Henry Kissinger.

The administrations of Franklin Roosevelt and the New Deal and later John Kennedy and Lyndon Johnson in particular with the "Great Society" continued to foster socialism on a war footing.

With Roosevelt, in order to make the NRA into a national effort comparable to that of a mobilization for war, they created symbols, techniques of advertising and ballyhoo, rallied cheering crowds, organized parades and mass meetings. The only thing missing was Leni Riefenstahl who had gained success with the filming of the 1934 Nazi Party rally. In the end, Dr. New Deal gave way to Dr. Win the War, and the social mobilization for war was already in place.

Conventional wisdom seeks to simplify our history and codify as doctrine what is, in fact, only a part of a much more complicated truth, and that truth is that American foreign policy has an interest in both realism and idealism, and always has. Jefferson shared Franklin's belief that idealism and realism should both play a role in foreign policy. In this nation our leaders are realists without illusion, or at least they should be if they are not. We must instill this nation with ideals and principles, while fully understanding that we cannot fall prey to illusion. We must believe without becoming cynical; we must be cynical without becoming cynics.

The debate over the fundamental question of what direction American foreign relations will take in the future seems to be an old one, as old as the country itself. Will the United States choose to play a continuing role in world affairs? The recent frustrations of American involvement in Somalia, Bosnia, Haiti, Afghanistan, and Iraq have shown that America's mission has been ill-defined. Merely standing for certain principles is insufficient. Now we face the task of trying to implement those principles in the hostile environment of the world outside of our own sovereignty.

History has always played an important role in finding answers or at least a certain wisdom necessary for guidance in involvement and intervention. Woodrow Wilson and William Jennings Bryan found themselves faced with the choice of imposing the will of the United States, through occupation and control, in the early days of their administration as they dealt with problems in Mexico and the Caribbean and other Latin American countries. Wilson abhorred the very thought of using force in international relations, yet he became the first president in American history to employ violent means upon nations that were somewhat free and sovereign.

In the words of Arthur S. Link, in his five-volume biography of Woodrow Wilson, "In all these episodes the story is remarkably the same in its larger outlines and meaning. It is one of men with noble motives being lured on by their own good intentions and sometimes by foolish or interested advisers, being influenced by subtle pressures and subconscious motivations that they did not recognize, and finally being trapped by events that they could not control. In short, it is a tale of what happened when evangels of democracy set out to teach other people how to elect good leaders and govern themselves well."[1]

At the end of the day, this nation must harken back to the words and the one principle of American foreign policy enunciated by John Quincy Adams, that while America is "the well-wisher to the freedom and independence of all," it is the "champion and vindicator only of her own."

Still it is important to remember the remainder of Adams's speech on July 4, 1820. Adams continued by saying that the Declaration of Independence was "the first solemn declaration by a nation of the only legitimate foundation of civil government. It was the cornerstone of a new fabric, destined to cover the surface of the globe…It stands, and must forever stand alone, a beacon on the summit of the mountain, to which all the inhabitants of the earth may turn their eyes for a genial and saving light till time shall be lost in eternity, and this globe itself dissolve, nor leave a wreck behind."

---

[1] Notes: A. S. Link, Wilson: The Struggle for Neutrality, Volume III (Princeton University Press, 1960, pp. 495–496.)

That "shining city on a hill" that "beacon on the summit of the mountain." From those early statements there has been a progression in the emergence of the American character and the parallel development of foreign policy. Beginning with the Puritans and their belief in especially the *Old Testament Christianity* of Robert Frost that recognizes the sanctity of the New Testament. Yet the Old-Testament Christians were able to see things from the Hebrew Bible's standpoint.

CHAPTER 14

The Age of Jackson

The America of Thomas Jefferson had begun to fade even before Jefferson was out of office. Change was inevitable. The economic and social climate was changing rapidly out of necessity and in actuality was betraying the dream of Jefferson's utopia.

Revolution was in the making during the decades that followed the War of 1812, and the nation seemed to be slipping back into one-party politics. Paradoxically, this one party-ism tended to create, without malice, a multiparty system, for in the absence of a strong opposition a regime tends to dissolve into numberless factions. The Federalist Party was dying because its leaders had elevated principle over party and in the end kept the former and lost the latter. The federalists left the republicans in control of a one-party government. In reality, the bad feelings in the politics of this time were not channeled into conflict between two national parties and hence were easily ignored.

It was left to Martin Van Buren to bring order to an indescribable situation of disorder. He knew that he must first knit Northern and Southern democrats, who had split from the parent Republican Party, behind Jackson who had immense personal popularity.

As Jackson became president, no one could have predicted that crisis would transform him into greatness, but Jackson's mind was two-sided. His intelligence expressed itself in judgment rather than analysis while his intellect, being a unique manifestation of human dignity, was forever dealing with the substance of things and for the meanings of situations as a whole. This was his strong point, for he was to become educated by the urgencies of the moment.

Jackson saw the necessity for strong executive leadership as an essential step in narrowing the gap between the people and the government and thus expanding the popular participation in the workings of democracy. In order to carry the fight to the people, Jackson needed followers who would remain strong on the economic front, for the central issue which faced his administration was not one of principles but one of power.

In Jackson's time, it was the nature of the conservative to view anything new with skepticism and to rely on that which was familiar and acceptable as though it were proven method. Jackson thus set out to destroy this as a myth.

The ancient preoccupations of economic life with equality, security, and productivity were narrowed down to a preoccupation with productivity and profit. The onerous interests of the business community were passed on as a social cure—all at the expense of an impoverished people. An economy dominated by individual responsibility was the ideal that the Jacksonians hoped to realize, but the advent of the corporation in industrialism brought about moral irresponsibility and depersonalization of economic life. In *The Age of Jackson*, Arthur M. Schlesinger Jr. writes, "With private conscience powerless, the only alternative to tyranny or anarchy was the growth of the public conscience, and the natural expression of the public conscience was the democratic government."

To Jackson then, the crucial question was not is "There too much government?" but, "Does the government promote too much the interests of a single group?" Jackson felt that he must serve the interests of the nation as a whole. This idea was expressed with acute realism and lucidity of judgment by Justice Roger Taney in his Charles River Bridge decision. He appealed to principles rather than precedents. It revealed a transition in the court as it drifted in the direction of narrowing the immunities of corporations and enlarging the scope of social legislation.

"The object and end of all government is to promote the happiness and prosperity of the community by which it is established; and it can never be assumed that the government intended to diminish its power of accomplishing this end for which it was created."

The startling implication was that Jeffersonian ideals required Hamiltonian means to achieve its ends. Strangely, the party of Jackson was based on Jeffersonian ideals, but Jackson soon realized that these ideals, in and of themselves, were inadequate to meet the needs of a country on the brink of social and economic revolution. The urgencies of the moment required also a political revolution and a party manned by men of democratic principle with the strength and vigor to see it through.

Following the War of Independence, the citizens of this country were to differ about matters that were of interest to all portions of the country equally. The general principles of government was the main concern, and thus the love of equality and independence was enough to arouse violent passions.

When the time came to lay the foundation of a new government, the nation found itself divided into two camps, according to Alexis De Tocqueville in *Democracy in America*. One camp wished to restrain the power of the people, while the other camp wished to extend it without limit. Some of the early leaders and Founding Fathers, such as John Adams, Alexander Hamilton, and others, sought to apply its doctrines to the constitution of the Union, wherein they were known and called federalists. The other party, championed by Jefferson and posing as the only party to love liberty, claimed the title republican.

Jackson was not a party man, but all of his instincts were leaning toward the republicans and their distrust of anyone who favored the wealthy and advocated the transfer of power from the states to the central government.

In 1859, Abraham Lincoln was amused to note that the party supposedly descended from Jefferson had stopped mentioning his name, while the party supposedly descended from his opponents was now draping itself in his mantle.

Jackson believed that those in authority must earn the respect of those Americans who placed them in office. In Jackson's day, honor was a core value for the vast majority of Americans. Americans from the very beginning of this nation have endeavored to stand on their dignity and rights. Politicians who condescend to their constituents will pay a price for their temerity.

Andrew Jackson had a unique set of principles of honor:

1) Respect
2) Equality
3) Individualism
4) Financial Esprit
5) Courage

Jackson lived by these principles, and he expected no less from those men around him and from the people of this country. Following the Battle of New Orleans in 1815 and a major defeat of the British in the War of 1812, the American people were swept up in a wave of patriotism that changed the character of the nation. People began to define themselves with the words "I am an American."

CHAPTER 15

The Question of Honor

The recent CPAC event has left me with some conclusions that may not do much for my reputation once I set them to paper. I have grown weary with the fact that we have allowed ourselves (conservative Christians) to be overwhelmed by the rhetoric of pusillanimous politicians who have no honor and show their contempt for the *bauble popularity*. Their attitude is that they say whatever they feel the present crowd would want to hear. They are pro-choice for one crowd and pro-life for another crowd. Where is the honor among these people?

Ann Coulter is the only one who tells it like it is and does not apologize for it. What she said about John Edwards needed to be said. I personally may have used a different choice of words, but if you listen to his speeches and some of the language he uses to put forth his positions, especially when he talks about America being a Christian nation, he is pandering to a specific group of people who resent Christianity. Her word was just what she said, a school yard taunt said in a humorous manner.

Then we have to listen to Alan Colmes, who serves only as a supercilious gadfly and is devoid of a useful purpose in life, berate Ann on the *H&C* show. I wish, like Zell Miller recently and Charles Gibson more than a century ago, that dueling was still legal. The reasons are listed below, and the account is taken from Doris Kearns Goodwin in her very fine book about Lincoln and his Cabinet, *Team of Rivals*.

We need some means of holding people to account when they attack our honor. It is not that I actually approve of dueling, but like Charles Gibson, the feeling is that something is missing in our public behavior. What is missing is honor.

Edward Bates was a congressman from Missouri when he got into a heated argument with fellow congressman George McDuffie of South Carolina on the floor of the house. McDuffie ridiculed him personally, and Bates, in an impulsive moment, challenged the South Carolinian to a duel. McDuffie, for reasons of his own, wisely declined the challenge and agreed to apologize for his offensive language. Some years later, reflecting on the Southern practice of the "code" of dueling, a friend of Edward Bates, Charles Gibson, maintained that as wicked as the code was, the vulgar public behavior following the demise of the practice was worse still. "The code preserved a dignity, justice and decorum that have since been lost," he argued, "to the great detriment of the professions, the public and the government. The present generation will think me barbarous but I believe that some lives lost in protecting the tone of the bar and the press, on which the republic itself so largely depends, are well spent."

The *code duello* was a long-standing practice for settling disputes among Southern gentlemen. The most infamous was the Hamilton-Burr duel which resulted in Hamilton's death and Burr's political fall. However, in the end it served the purpose of maintaining honor.

Chivalry was and is a part of the Southern heritage and deserves closer attention than it has received in the past. It was an institution of strong and, on the whole, good influence. It was not strange that a chivalric code should develop in the South since chivalry has been one of the main traditions of European civilization and the South was always disposed to accept rather than reject European institutions.

"All the antiquated concern for 'honor' smacks of a bit too much concern for what we would call 'self-image' or 'ego.' As someone said, humility is not thinking less of yourself, it's less thinking of yourself." This is one of the criticisms of honor. I do not in any way agree with criticism and must consider the source.

Honor has to do with protecting your good name and reputation. When it is besmirched by those who lie with impunity, what recourse do you have within the legal system unless you can prove libel? And that is very difficult. As I said earlier, humility must come before honor, and the lack of honor in our society is evident. Humility then is also in very short supply.

Joe Wilson and Valerie Plame lied with impunity, and Libby ends up paying for it. Where is the justice?

Hillary Clinton, whose middle name is impunity, can lie like no other when she speaks before a Black church gathering and fakes a Black accent while reciting the words of a James Cleveland gospel song. How dare she. Her campaign and that of Barack Obama are beginning to sound like the old *Amos 'n' Andy* show, and we all know who the *kingfish* is.

Proverbs 15:33 states, "Respect, for the Lord will teach you wisdom."

If you want to be honored, you must be humble.

Honor is not an antiquated concern; it is what is lacking in our children, who show no respect as commanded by God in "Honor thy father and mother." In our world dominated by moral relativism, no one is accountable for their actions.

First Samuel 2:30 says, "So the Lord, the God of Israel, says: I promised that your family and your ancestor's family would serve me always. But now the Lord says: This must stop! I will honor those who honor me, but I will dishonor those who ignore me."

Honor is not an antiquated concern; it is an essential concern. It speaks of the very essence of humanity. Without honor, we are barbarous.

There is a concerted effort by our agenda-driven society to tear down our institutions that are basically Judeo-Christian values and install a secular humanist system of morals and philosophy which is, in the words of Winston Churchill, "as malevolent as Christianity was benevolent, which, if not arrested would shatter irretrievably all that Christianity has rendered possible."

There are those who seem to obfuscate the issues rather than enlighten. Hence, the supercilious gadfly syndrome. Dr. Martin Luther King Jr. wrote this in his *Letter from Birmingham Jail.*

"Shallow understanding from people of goodwill is more frustrating than absolute misunderstanding from people of ill will."

I absolutely believe that any effective grassroots movement *must* be united and resolved around some narrow and specific objectives. This will take strong, principled, and dedicated leadership. However, we are simply wasting our time and energy, in my opinion, if we focus only on electing *fresh*, new political leaders or on forming a new political party. Our unified, focused, and resolved objective *must* be, first and foremost, the recapture of those institutions which shape the hearts and minds of the American people! And I believe it all begins with the retaking of the stronghold of education.

Some years after the constitution had been ratified by the several states, James Bryce, a British statesman who served as Britain's ambassador to the United States from 1907 to 1913 and a keen observer of the American Republic and its form of government, noted that "America is all of a piece, its institutions are a product of its economic and social conditions, an expression of its character." That is to say that the republic, its rule by law and reliance on principles that do not change, is not a cause but an effect of our national character.

Their battle cry can be heard on almost every college campus in America: "Hey, hey, ho, ho, Western culture has got to go." This chant was heard in the campus of Stanford University some years ago. The leader of this group was none other than Jesse Jackson.

The liberal Left refuses to acknowledge that our unity arises from an ideology and value system that is more right of center than they are willing to admit. They wish to take away our unalienable rights and replace them with a fascist ideology very similar to socialism or communism. They like to call it secular humanism, but it is still fascism in that it denies the reality of a supreme being who grants us those unalienable human rights.

All of the agendas of the liberal Left have a common link. They seek to gain power through the reversal of human norms, natural law, and the social institutions so necessary for the continuance of freedom and democracy in America. It is a malignancy filled system of philosophy comparable to *black magic*.

Finally, the ACLU in particular is a major carrier of this infectious disease as they mount attacks on each and every aspect of religious and individual expression in our daily lives. They seek only to enslave, not to defend, our freedoms.

Social justice agendas have been launched in the name of civil rights and other rights that exist only in the minds of nine (not all nine) unelected justices of the Supreme Court with the sole purpose of creating in America a cultural revolution in which God no longer dominates the moral horizon and personal autonomy and individual choice become the twin pillars of a debased moral view.

Ambitious to excel, to make himself known, John Adams had nonetheless recognized at an early stage that happiness came not from fame and fortune, *and all such things*, but from *a habitual contempt of them.* He prized the Roman ideal of honor yet realized that fame without honor would be "like a faint meteor gliding through the sky, shedding only transient light."

In Philippians 2, Paul uses Rome's *cursus honorum* to intentionally structure his portrayal of Jesus with Roman social values and practices in view.

CHAPTER 16

---- ❧ ----

The Need for Christian Soldiers

Progressivism, Fascism, and the Feminist Movement

Some have made the assertion that Islam was *born in the full light of history*. That statement is incorrect since *the full light* is but the reflected glimmer of medieval Muslim scholars, men who themselves were believers and, therefore, of necessity, apologists. It is time to take a stand. It is time for Christians to stand up and say that accountability is necessary and essential. It is time for Christian churches and ministers to preach sound doctrine, to preach the truth and defend the truth against all attacks. They must understand that their job is to proudly deliver what Christ, the apostles, and the prophets have proclaimed in the gospel of Jesus Christ as it was given to them. Nothing taken away; nothing added. They must deliver the package.

I am sure that you have heard it said that "September 11 changed America forever." That is a given, but nowhere do we hear a definitive and coherent explanation of just what, exactly, changed. What changed other than the fact that we, Americans, were attacked on our own soil? For the first time in American history, we have been forced to confront an Islamic militancy that has been assaulting the rest of the world for almost fourteen centuries. This advice is taken from the article by Michael Medved on August 16, 2006, "Does U.S. Bigotry Cause Muslim Madness?":

> The best way to respond to aggressive, triumphalist religiosity from the Muslim community isn't to insist on more tolerance, or even acceptance, of Islamic demands; nor can we hope to counteract the allure of Jihadist ideology with ringing affirmations of easy-going secularism. Given the deep-seated human hunger for connection with a Supreme Being, the nearly universal yearning to draw closer to eternal truth, it's not possible to beat something (radical Islam) with nothing (secular agnosticism). In this sense, the United States, with our robust movement of Christian revival, counts as far better equipped for the struggle ahead than our European allies where traditional faith of all kinds (except for Islam) has largely collapsed. Even skeptics and non-believers ought to welcome the vigor of Christian evangelism as the most effective counterweight to fundamentalist Islam. If those three British bomb plot suspects who converted to Islam had instead found their way to Pentecostal Christianity, or traditional Catholicism, or the Church of Jesus Christ, Latter-Day Saints, would they ever have considered killing themselves to blow planes out of the sky?

The problem with Muslim communities in the United States and Europe isn't that they face discrimination from their neighbors; it's that they receive dysfunctional, delusional teaching in too many of their own mosques. And the way to overcome that teaching isn't to demand more respect from infidel nonbelievers, but to respond to the Islamic challenge with an energetic assertion of more positive and productive religious alternatives; namely, Christianity.

This assassination of our American character is indicative of the fact that we must free ourselves from the grip of atheistic humanism, secular humanism, and Enlightenment conspirators, who have attempted to replace our Christian attitude and strength in this country, as they have in Europe, with a system of morals and philosophy which, in the words of Winston Churchill, is, "as malevolent as Christianity was benevolent, which, if not arrested would shatter irretrievably all that Christianity has rendered possible." This malignant worldview "has been the mainspring of every subversive movement during the nineteenth century. This worldwide conspiracy for the overthrow of civilization and the reconstitution of society on the basis of arrested development, of envious malevolence, and impossible equality has been steadily growing."

The *God-is-dead* community uses a deceptive code to cover the true meaning of their words. In a study funded in 2003 by taxpayers to the tune of $1.2 million, the National Institute of Mental Health and the National Science Foundation stated, essentially, that traditionalists are mentally disturbed, that social conservatives suffer from mental rigidity, dogmatism, and uncertainty avoidance, together with associated indicators for mental illness. After the deceptions are uncovered we can find that *dogmatism* refers to Christianity, *mental rigidity* refers to individualism, and the psycho-babble term *uncertainty avoidance* really means that Christians are resistant to the erasing of Christianity by means of a process of consensus.

Individualism that Christianity gives rise to is most devastating to the atheistic, global collectivists. John Dewey and his progressive education system is threatened by high literacy rates, and they fear that teaching children to read was a perversion and the sustaining force behind individualism. It stands as the great bulwark against the collectivist efforts of socialism and atheistic humanism.

The feminist movement has done more to destroy and distort the natural roles that distinguish men and women with their agenda that seems more intent on domination than on the equal rights that they claim to desire. They have added a violence to the program that includes lying. They insist on promoting these lies which do nothing more than perpetuate their movement and keep them in feminist's jobs. Feminism is a self-perpetuating movement. If they ever achieved their stated goals, they would then have to seek real employment.

There are those in the feminist movement who still promote the idea of an ideological oppression of women, and yet all of the evidence would indicate that the male of the species is the endangered one.

The boys and young men of today need help in academics. They need to catch up with the girls. They need the same love and discipline and understanding that the male youth of an earlier generation received. They do not need to be rescued from masculinity, but instead they need to be taught the meaning of manhood by strong role models, increased expectation of maturity, and greater spiritual preparation. Rather than going from teen to adulthood, there is an extended adolescence which delays that maturity sometimes indefinitely.

The idea of Christian individualism takes on a new meaning and makes good sense in a world filled with too many people who say, "Look at me, look at me." Evidently the Obama and Clinton campaigns are examples of flagrant narcissism.

To understand Barack Obama, you need to go back to his time as a community organizer in Chicago where he was trained by Saul Alinsky's disciples and followers. As you probably know, both he and Hillary Clinton have strong ties to Alinsky and his *Rules for Radicals*. Clinton has a long history of attraction to radicals and radical groups such as the Black Panthers, Alinsky, and some would claim Yasir Arafat. Basically you are looking at two candidates on the democratic side who are both dangerous radicals with radical ideas for social and human reconstruction. Obama is by far the most dangerous. First off, his campaign is not being run by him, but by people who are smarter than he is. They understand Obama and his unbridled love of power.

Alinsky's worldview is distinctly fascistic, not too different from that of life defined by war, contests of power, the imposition of will and shares a foundational hostility to dogma.

The desired end of the movement is what Alinsky regards as the source of life's meaning. Ours "is a world not of angels but of angles," he proclaims in *Rules for Radicals*, "where men speak of moral principles but act on power principles." Alinsky's method of community organizing, according to Jonah Goldberg in his book *Liberal Fascism*, borrowed tactics from the Catholic Church, Al Capone's mobsters, University of Chicago sociologist, and John L. Lewis's union organizers.

The apostle Paul's rhetorical skills are never better than when he abstains from using them and boasts of folly and feebleness. In this way he admonishes us to be a fool for Christ.

The Christian civilization of the Middle Ages taught European man his own dignity. It taught an emerging Europe a proper respect for individualism, in sharp contrast to Islam. I fear now that they have lost that dignity and strength of character. No one knows what they believe anymore. They don't seem to believe in an afterlife, so where are all of the Christian defenders? I fear that Europe is already lost. Where is a leader to come from, a strong leader, the likes of Charlemagne?

The Christian idea of vocation, that unique role that each Christian plays in the cosmic drama of creation and redemption, is the one root of the Western idea of individualism. It was not, in its origins, a matter of self-constituting autonomy but of living out the singular, God-given destiny that is every human life.

Moreover, the Christian doctrines of the incarnation (God entering history in the flesh) and the redemption ("God so loved the world that he gave his only Son...not to condemn the world, but that the world might be saved through him" [John 3:16–17]) gave the world a dignity it could not achieve by its own efforts. Worldliness, in the Christian sense of the term, can have a noble meaning: the core Western conviction about history—that the human story is not just one thing after another—was deeply influenced by Christian doctrine.

Thomas Jefferson is often, more often than not, described as conflicted in his understanding of democracy, but upon further investigation there are completely different and unexpected new layers of light, dark, and in-between in the social vision of Thomas Jefferson. It is totally possible to reposition Jefferson's ideal of self-government so that it reflects what is actually an eye-opening teaching about the power of community.

The Jeffersonian social ideal actually requires beforehand and supports an exceptional inner struggle on the part of the individual. Understanding Jefferson's ideal anew and wiping away liberalism and the liberal media clichés regarding the ideals and standards of communal relationship, we begin to take on entirely new meanings. Once this is accomplished, the ideal of democracy begins to seem more like an outline for men and women searching for conscious individuality. Not a pattern that we are supposed to conform to and obey.

Jefferson's vision is not the secular form of individuality where everyone gets what he or she wants, rather a life which corresponds to an individual's will. It is more in the form of the individualism that Christianity teaches. For Jefferson, the aim of self-government is not the satisfaction of desires, but the incarnation of our free will. This is the true meaning of freedom.

The *Tao Te Ching*, the ancient book of China from Chuang Tzu, is the world's most famous and influential blending of spiritual wisdom and political intelligence. Our country needs leadership and leaders of mythic proportions, not leaders who wish to enslave us with their ideas of "the politics of meaning" and "it takes a village" which is ultimately, as Jonah Goldberg explains, a theocratic doctrine because it seeks to answer the fundamental questions about existence, argues that they can only be answered collectively, and insists that the state puts those answers into practice. Listen to the words of Chuang Tzu and hear the Christianity of Thomas Merton:

> *If the sage would guide the people, he must serve*
> *with humility.*
> *If he would lead them, he must follow behind.*
> *In this way when the sage rules, the people will not*
> *feel oppressed.*
> *When he stands before them, they will not be*
> *harmed.*
> *The whole world will support him and will not tire*
> *of him.*

Because he does not compete,
He does not meet competition.

Better stop short than fill to the brim.
Oversharpen the blade, and the edge will soon blunt.
Amass a store of gold and jade, and no one can pro-
*   tect it.*
Claim wealth and titles, and disaster will follow.
Retire when the work is done.
This is the way of heaven.

The Leadership of Jimmy Carter and the Leftist Legacy

It is said time and again that September 11, 2001, changed our country and the world forever. The truth of the matter is that the true nature of Islam reared its evil head and unleashed fourteen centuries of hatred. They are still fighting the crusades. They continue to hate the infidel who caused their defeat centuries ago. So many of the problems that we face today, both internally and externally, both domestic and foreign, have their origins in the 1960s and the 1970s, particularly with the presidency of Jimmy Carter.

Our Nobel Peace Prize-winning ex-president, Jimmy Carter, along with the two senators from Massachusetts, the late "Lion of the Senate" Edward (Ted) Kennedy and John Kerry, should have been tried for treason. There are plenty of reasons for this trial to become a reality. There were intrusions into foreign policy by Kennedy talking with the KGB during the Carter and Reagan presidencies. However, let us deal with Jimmy Carter first since the leftist legacy began with him, in large part.

It is not just his policy of appeasement and his attempts to turn militant Islam into a tool of foreign policy, but together with his portentous national security adviser, Zbigniew Brzezinski, they created an international network, with secretly authorized funds of $500 million, that would serve to spread Islamism in Central Asia and therefore *destabilize* the Soviet Union. The CIA called this "Operation

Cyclone," and in the following years poured over $4 billion into setting up Islamic training schools in Pakistan (hence the Taliban movement, which means "student"). The result of their *opprobriums* has been considerably more formidable than "a few stirred-up Muslims."

I include this excerpt in order to show what happens when we get the leadership we deserve, not the leadership that we need. Carter poses as a Christian, and yet he exemplifies a total lack of the American character, which is essentially a Christian product. Our national character will determine whether our politics is good or bad. The republic, its rule by law and reliance on principles that do not change, is not a cause but an effect of our national character. Our people must not allow the American character to be compromised. Instead it must be revitalized and made strong again. Christianity must be the leader in this effort.

A strong electorate will send a strong message that those who wish to lead must also be willing to follow.

"The interest of the man must be connected with the constitutional rights of the place." To Madison, government was the greatest of all reflections on human nature. If men were angels, no government would be necessary. Christianity is not a series of truths in the plural, but rather truth spelled with a capital 'T.' Truth about total reality, not just about religious things. Biblical Christianity is Truth concerning total reality and the intellectual holding of that Total Truth and then living in the light of that Truth."

Alexander Solzhenitsyn also said, "The line separating good and evil passes not through states, nor between classes, nor between political parties either, but right through every human heart—and through all human hearts."

Living in the light of total truth

In the past I have written much about *individualism* and the second commandment, "to love one's neighbor as oneself." Christianity teaches individualism as seen in the radical command of Jesus Christ to love God totally with heart and soul and mind and strength. The second commandment is to love one's neighbor as oneself and as such can only be sustained through courage and with a unique blend of faith and freedom. It is only the second commandment, because what makes sin most heinous in the first place is its offensiveness to God. God is always the most offended party. It follows then that the first sin is the failure to love God with heart and soul and mind and strength. What is it then that prevents us from loving God totally with heart, soul, mind, and strength?

With the growing strength of secular humanism and their agenda to instill a dualistic thought process of nature/grace or the divide between fact/value along with the rise of Darwinism and his naturalistic mechanism for the origin of life comes the notion that reason is religiously neutral. Secularism and naturalism are falsely promoted as being neutral while biblical views are dismissed as biased private opinions. The desired effect of secular or atheistic humanism is that Christians will abandon the world of ideas and the Christian worldview to the secularists.

Walker Percy, in *Love in the Ruins* (1978), speaks of the "dread chasm that has rent the soul of Western man ever since the famous philosopher Descartes ripped body loose from mind and turned the very soul into a ghost that haunts its own house."

This was the beginning of secular dualism. Following Rousseau and Enlightenment, Descartes and the duality of mind and matter, Kant wrote, it is "necessary that everything which takes place should be infallibly determined in accordance with the laws of nature." Today, the most common expression of this dualism is fact versus value.

Returning to the quote from Francis Schaeffer which destroys secular dualism, he states that Christianity fulfills both our reason and our spiritual yearnings. It provides the world with a unified truth. Einstein long searched for a unified field theory, but science was unable to prove that theory. Christianity has provided the answer with "Biblical Christianity is truth concerning total reality and the intellectual holding of that total truth and then living in the light of that truth." Man may be led to believe that he is nothing more than a machine, but his whole life is a denial of that belief.

Nothing is preexisting or eternal except God. The three-part grid of creation, fall, and redemption must be seen in balance and with no emphasis on one or the other. There can be no split that divides a person's inner life.

Living in the light of that truth is how you love God totally with whole heart, whole soul, whole mind, and whole strength. It is important to acknowledge the God of the Bible in both words and in practice. One without the other and "an equal inhumanity will result." According to Paul in Romans chapter 2, "For it is not those who hear the law who are righteous in God's sight, but it is those who obey the law who will be declared righteous." By removing the absolutes, *liberalism* has led to a reversal of human norms and natural law while we have fallen into a wilderness of *moral relativism*.

The Homosexual Agenda

Agendas have a common link and a common purpose. That purpose is to create a society wherein the natural distinctions between male and female are dissolved. That purpose is to destroy true academic freedom by not allowing other theories except evolution to be taught to our children. That purpose is to establish an atheistic society by making law for the sake of the antichrist. That purpose is to socially indoctrinate our children and destroy our Christian heritage. That purpose is to blur the existence of God and, with His existence, the explanations in His Word. Without His Word there is no intellectually honest basis for what is man, what gives meaning, or what are absolute morals. Without this God and man's understanding of Him, the human being will always go for substitutes: idols as visible gods, ideologies as master plans for life, personal meaning for the moment, and relative morals for personal desires. Thus creating cultural and moral anarchy. This is how this phenomenon must be viewed. This agenda-driven society controlled by evolutionary secular humanism is determined to create cultural and moral anarchy.

Each agenda is extremely well organized with specific goals and a plan of attack. The gay agenda was put forth by homosexual activists in their *1972 Gay Rights Platform*. The 1972 Gay Rights Platform reveals two of the central demands of, as Matt Barber describes them, "the homosexual lobby's lavender curtain."

One, "Repeal all laws governing the age of sexual consent." As you can see, this opens up our children and teens to pedophiles and homosexuals who wish to prey on them.

Two, "Repeal all legislative provisions that restrict the sex or number of persons entering into a marriage unit." This is an all-out attempt to redefine marriage so that all objections to any conceivable combination are rendered with having no practical significance.

CHAPTER 17

──── ⟡ ────

Enemies of Freedom

Some have said that Freud, Marx, Charles Darwin, and John Dewey have been the leading cause of social indoctrination and mental confusion in young boys and girls, who not long ago were looked upon in a sentimental fashion as *angels* or as *innocents*. Thanks to Freud and his followers, boys and girls are understood to have complicated inner lives; to feel love, hate, envy, and rivalry in various and subtle mixtures; to be eager participants in the sexual and emotional politics of the home, neighborhood, and school. Yet most parents still cling to the notion of childhood innocence in another way. We do not see that our children make ethical decisions every day in their own lives or realize how attuned they may be to moral currents and issues in the larger society.

Now we must add other names to the list of enemies of freedom: Saul Alinsky and his gang of community organizers, most notably Barack Obama and Hillary Rodham Clinton. The Clintons, both Bill and Hillary, will use any means to win. They hold to the progressive idea of historical contingency, which means that each period of history is guided by different and unique values that change over time. The *self-evident truths* that the founders upheld in the Declaration of Independence, including natural rights, are no longer applicable.

Circumstances, not eternal principles, ultimately dictate justice, according to the progressive idea of historical contingency. The founders recognized man's capacity for evil and saw the need for fixed and universal principles that do not change. Progressives do not fear man's capacity for evil; they believe that properly enlightened human beings could be entrusted with power and not abuse it. The *elites* shall rule the rest of us and will not abuse their power. That is why Alinsky dedicated his book to Lucifer as the first radical. Now we have the continuing fight between good and evil, and it is up to us to recognize the difference.

As Frank Goodnow describes in *The American Conception of Liberty*, the rights which man possesses are, it is believed, conferred upon him, not by his Creator, but rather by the society to which he belongs. What they are is to be determined by the legislative authority in the view of the needs of that society. Social expediency, rather than natural right, is thus to determine the sphere of individual freedom of action. This is the world that Hillary Clinton and Barack Obama have created for us. It is called tyranny, and we must oppose it with all that is within us, or this republic will go the way of other free nations of history.

Sociology is the descriptive pseudo-science that disguises its uncertainties in statistical mists as it battens on the narrow gap of information between psychology and anthropology. The kind of nonmajor that so many Americans use to justify their four-year intellectual vacations is designed to prolong adolescence. "Honor your father and your mother, that your days may be long upon the land which the Lord your God is giving you." How do children acquire moral values? They learn from their parents. Parenting is a huge responsibility not to be taken lightly.

In the world of today, we find our family bonds, our traditions, our religious beginnings, our Founding Fathers' legacy, our institutions that bolster us in a time of doubt and uncertainty coming under attack from a cultural deviancy that has its roots in a core group of intellectuals from 1920s in Germany. It is known as the Frankfurt School, formed in Germany in 1923 by a group of intellectuals. They were the forebears of what has come to be known as cultural Marxism, a radical social movement that has transformed American culture. It is commonly known today as political correctness. This small group of German intellectuals devised concepts, processes, and action plans which were implemented so quietly that the American people were unaware of the changes that were taking place in our everyday lives. There was no force involved, but our liberty has been rerouted from "We the People" to a statist politico bent on ruling through tyranny.

"They make a desert and they call it peace," said Tacitus.

More than one such instance of this transformation began during the Woodrow Wilson administration with his closest confidante and adviser, Edward Mandell House. Colonel House, as he was to become known, was Wilson's most intimate and influential adviser and is credited with orchestrating Wilson's presidential nomination. House played an important role as campaign strategist first getting the nomination for Wilson and then the presidency. However, the principal person responsible for Wilson's election was Theodore Roosevelt who, because of an insatiable craving for power, ran as a Progressive Party (Bull Moose) candidate. This split the opposition to Wilson and ensured a democratic victory.

The administrative state in America traces its origins to the progressive movement and in particular theories inspired by the German political philosopher Wilhelm Friedrich Hegel. Progressives like Woodrow Wilson believed that the development of the modern state marked an *end of history*, a point at which there is no longer any need for conflict over fundamental principles. Politics at this point would give way to administration, and administration becomes the domain not of partisans, but of neutral and highly trained experts. Colonel House wrote a book called *Phillip Dru: Administrator* subtitled *A Story of Tomorrow*, 1920–1935.

According to Mazzini, "No war of classes, no hostility to existing wealth, no wanton or unjust violation of the rights of property, but a constant disposition to ameliorate the condition of the classes least favored by fortune."

This book is dedicated to the unhappy many who have lived and died lacking opportunity, because, in the starting, the worldwide social structure was wrongly begun.

The story of Phillip Dru has carried far beyond 1935 and into present day. This is the making of the enemies of freedom. Woodrow

Wilson was the beginning of the progressive era along with Theodore Roosevelt. Since that time freedom and liberty have become the targets of the liberal progressives who wish to control our lives in every aspect, as seen in the present day with the advent of the Affordable Care Act or "Obama Care" as it is now known. The inclusion of the Internal Revenue Service into the administration of this ignoble act is another step toward tyranny by the administration of Barack Hussein Obama. John Ransom wrote a story entitled "The Obama Story" and states, "Let's start where it first began." He goes on to say not with the election of Obama, but it was when Obama started lobbing missiles at Libya, while the liberals assured us that we were not at war. Instead the administration described it as time-limited, scope-limited, kinetic military activity, which is just another made-up phrase that liberals use to remind us that they are the people Orwell warned us about.

Critical theory is the coy self-description of the ideological Left (progressivism). It is defined by the total rejection of the existing social order. It is the movement that undermines the character of the American people and attempts to deny us as a Christian nation. It is a cultural deviancy that has come to be known as cultural Marxism, and it has been on the move since the 1920s. It is commonly known today as political correctness. It must be stopped. We cannot afford to lose our Judeo Christian identity. Once that happens, this republic, as we know it, will be doomed.

Theodore Roosevelt stated, "It is not the critic who counts; not the man who points out how the strong man stumbles, or where the doer of deeds could have done them better. The credit belongs to the man who is actually in the arena, whose face is marred by dust and sweat and blood; who strives valiantly; who errs, who comes short again and again, because there is no effort without error and shortcoming; but who does actually strive to do the deeds; who knows great enthusiasms, the great devotions; who spends himself in a worthy cause; who at the best knows in the end the triumph of high achievement, and who at the worst, if he fails, at least fails while daring greatly, so that his place shall never be with those cold and timid souls who neither know victory nor defeat."

CHAPTER 18

On the Virtues of Intolerance

Diversity as a United Front Against Conservatism

Those who claim to have a "live-and-let-live" philosophy are either fooling themselves or are fooled by the radical Left and the media hype spewed almost daily by the liberal press. How do you live and let live when those whom you are allowing to live thusly are busily building organizations that have political agendas that are by design aimed at denying you your right to *live* as you would *let them live*? This philosophy leads to anarchy and nothing else.

There can no longer be a body of people who refuses to take a stand in the face of moral decay. Those who would allow secular corruption of our children by not allowing prayer in school, by not allowing the Ten Commandments to be displayed, by proclaiming that any display of the birth of Christ in the form of a manger scene on the courthouse lawn or public school grounds or any public property is an establishment of religion are not only wrong but dangerous and deliberate.

We can no longer be tolerant of judges and politicians who wish to destroy our constitution and our reliance on old identities. They must be revitalized and reaffirmed, not blurred and compromised. We, as Christians, in order to survive, need to rediscover theological firmness and doctrinal clarity.

"Hey, hey, ho, ho, Western Culture has got to go." This chant was heard in the campus of Stanford University some years ago. The leader of this group of protesting students was none other than Jesse Jackson. They, of course, were not referring to the teaching of History of Western Civilization 101 in the freshman year.

Diversity is a dangerous metaphor for division, confusion, and mediocrity. College students fall prey to what G. K. Chesterton said about people, "When people stop believing in God, they don't believe in nothing, they believe in anything."

Diversity programs and sensitivity training are sold by the multicultural activists as the great equalizer while it is really the grand promoter of mediocrity, the enemy of excellence and individual achievement. It is *bogus*, in the words of the author of *Illiberal Education* Dinesh D'Souza, "that it does not reflect the temper or the accomplishment of other cultures but a distorted and prejudicial view of Western culture." He continues by saying that "Multicultural education, in general, is inspired by political activists who are alienated from what they see to be the racism, the sexism, and the homophobia of the West."

It is bogus in that the multicultural activists do not like what they see abroad so they look to nonrepresentative figures, figures who do not reflect the temper or the accomplishment of their own cultures, but who reflect the political prejudices of Western culture. Yet it is being fed to us with a shovel as politically correct. This way we do not offend anyone, yet it takes away that very right of free speech that the ACLU claims to be defending.

One example of this bogus attempt to distort and create a prejudicial view of Western culture is the 1992 Nobel Peace Prize winner, Rigoberta Menchu Tum. Research into her background revealed that she had been lying all along. The story that informed of Rigoberta's secular sainthood came apart following the research carried out by Anthropologist David Stoll. His research, confirmed by the *New York Times* and reported by Nathanael Blake in his article on April 21, 2006, revealed that she was not illiterate; she had been educated in a prestigious Catholic boarding school. The land dispute that was considered central to her formulating her Marxist beliefs did not put her family against wealthy landowners. It was actually against their own relatives. Other facts included in the report stated that her brother Nicolas did not die of starvation but was alive and well in Guatemala. It does not matter if these are lies; her lies are noble, according to her supporters, for the normal standards of historical accuracy do not apply since her falsehoods supposedly served a good cause.

Radical Islam is just what the doctor ordered. It is what multiculturalism has been waiting for all along. The beauty of multiculturalism is that you can choose which side of the war you want to fight on. Either *for* or *against*, whichever one fits for the moment. The Michael Moores of the world speak with disdain about the America that they live in and then proceed to take advantage of each and every aspect of our culture that makes them wealthier than they deserve. They are un-American and traitors, and yet our leaders refuse to brand them as such, proclaiming this as a fine example of the virtues of the multicultural state. Our leaders congratulate themselves on the boundless tolerance that this republic affords even as the forces of the multicultural activists and ideologues consume this republic.

Multicultural education is too important to leave in the hands of the activists and ideologues. They tend to divide rather than unite. We live in a multiracial society, and we should be looking for the commonality of all Americans. Those traits that we share in common as Americans, not as African American, Arab American, or Mexican Americans, but as Americans without divided loyalties. We now see *illegal* Mexicans and members of the Hispanic community carrying Mexican flags and signs claiming that Europeans are illegal and have been since 1492. Their aim is not *immigration*, per se (which has long been provided by the United States through legal means), but anarchy.

The liberal Left refuses to acknowledge that our unity arises from an ideology and value system that is more right of center than they are willing to admit.

The war on terror is what we have chosen to call this challenge to our freedom, but we continue to sleepwalk while our culture is being systematically destroyed from within. Since the crusades, Islam has tried to portray themselves as victims of religious persecution when in reality it was an excuse for four centuries of conquest.

There has been no hijacking of a beautiful religion as President Bush was always trying to tell the American people. Look around you and you will see in every part of the world Christians being killed by Islam in the name of Allah. The house of Islam is in a state of permanent war, and the choice of conversion or death is the only option offered to Christians and Jews. It is an ideology, not a religion. It is a race and an ideology totally alien to God that has invaded the land of Christians, and we must defeat this radical Islamist ideology just as we defeated the Soviet communist ideology and Nazism and Adolf Hitler's brand of anti-Semitism.

Muslim aggression has all through history been and continues to be "Jihad without end." The Muslim does not hate us because they hate freedom; they hate us because we are not Muslim. It is a religious crusade to create a Muslim world dominated by Islam. This is not new; it was going on long before Pope Urban II declared that "A race absolutely alien to God has invaded the land of Christians, has reduced the people with sword, rapine and flame." The pope continued by stating, "On whom, therefore, does the task lie of avenging this, of redeeming this situation, if not on you, upon whom above all nations God has bestowed outstanding glory in arms, magnitude of heart, litheness of body and strength to humble anyone who resists you."

There is no substitute for victory, and this is the attitude that we must maintain if we are to defeat *terrorism*. We cannot wait for Islam to be reformed or to win the hearts and minds of the mullahs. They view diplomacy and negotiation as a sign of weakness.

Jerusalem is sacred to the Muslim belief as the city from which the prophet Muhammad ascended into heaven, but if the God of Christianity is correct in His teachings through Jesus Christ as all Christians throughout the world believe, then Muhammad, along with Abu Musab al-Zarqawi and the nineteen Muslims who flew airplanes into the World Trade Center, the Pentagon, and a field in Pennsylvania, are in hell where they belong. They are despicable, thieves, liars, dirty, awful without a redeeming feature, not martyrs.

Their mind-set on "Jihad without end" leaves no room for negotiation or diplomacy. Perhaps we, as Christians, should offer Muslims the same alternative they offer to the Christian world: convert or die. I fully understand that this notion defies true Christian belief, but if Christianity is to survive, then the issue of self-defense is an undeniable fact of life.

CHAPTER 19

—— ⁓ ——

Understanding Obama

Liberalism in Its Most Pernicious Form

In order to understand Barack Obama, you must understand Saul Alinsky and his *Rules for Radicals*. As Jonah Goldberg points out, Alinsky's worldview is distinctly fascistic. Welcome to the world of *Il Duce* Benito Mussolini. Life is defined by war, contests of power, the imposition of will and shares a bedrock hostility to dogma. Alinsky believes in only the desired ends of the movement, which he regards as the source of life's meaning. What comes through most is his unbridled love of power. Power is good in its own right. Ours "is a world not of angels but of angles," he proclaims in *Rules for Radicals*, "where men speak of moral principles but act on power principles." Alinsky's method of community organizing borrowed tactics from the Catholic Church, Al Capone's mobsters, University of Chicago sociologists, and John L. Lewis's union organizers.

Alinsky dedicated his book to the one that he calls the very first radical: Lucifer, "the first radical known to man who rebelled against the establishment and did it so effectively that he at least won his own kingdom."

There is a dilemma that we, in a free society, face when black and white is not clear and varying shades of gray appear to isolate the black and white. Finding moral clarity becomes far more difficult. It is very easy for those of us living in a free society to lose moral clarity.

In the collective society, the primary challenge is finding the inner strength to confront evil. In the free world, the primary challenge is finding the moral clarity to see evil. If your core values are in place, here then is your greatest strength.

It is a world not of angels, but of angles. It is called *reconciliation*; one side gets the power while the other side gets reconciled to it. Obama played the same dirty game in his Illinois Senate race and against Jack Ryan. Obama is nothing more than a street thug.

If you read his autobiography, *Dreams from My Father: A Story of Race and Inheritance*, you will readily see that Obama hates the fact that he is half-White. He goes out of his way to discover his interior self, which he considers to be only Black. A Black American who deliberately separated himself from his multiracial heritage in order to give himself a hundred-percent Black persona, different and alienated from the White world around him. With his new all-Black identity, Obama stews about injustices that he never personally experienced and feeds his warped worldview by withdrawing into a "smaller and smaller coil of rage." He lives with a *nightmare vision* of Black powerlessness.

Obama says that the hate doesn't go away. "It formed a counter-narrative buried deep within each person and at the center of which stood white people—some cruel, some ignorant, sometimes a single face, sometimes just a faceless image of a system claiming power over our lives." No matter how much of this hatred was influenced by his father and others, it was further learned at the church he chose to attend for twenty years. That is the church in Chicago headed by the Reverend Jeremiah Wright.

Obama's worldview sees United States history as a consistent tale of oppressors and oppressed. He objects to the public schools because Black kids are learning "someone else's history, someone else's culture." These are all quotes from the book, his autobiography.

William Ayers and his terrorist wife are even more sinister now than they were in their Weatherman days. "The Christian idea of vocation, that unique role that each Christian plays in the cosmic drama of creation and redemption, is the one root of the Western idea of individualism. It was not, in its origins, a matter of self-constituting autonomy but of living out the singular, God-given destiny that is every human life."

The new education of today rests on two intellectual pillars: its use or misuse of science and its appeal to the educational philosophy of John Dewey.

The objectives of Dewey's educational theory and his general philosophy was that of the development of an educational theory that would be wholly consistent with Darwinism and the Origin of Species. In this sense Dewey saw education as a major force in social reconstruction.

While reading Ayers's books that he has written on education, you find that the major thrust is not education of a child's mind but the social indoctrination and social reconstruction beginning at a very early age. Teachers no longer are required to know their subject; they must, however, be well trained in the methods of teaching socialist indoctrination.

The high-risk subprime mortgage social engineering community service experiment by left-wing ACORN and Obama has created the largest financial crisis since the Great Depression. The full reach of the corruption and scandal may never be known, but those who created it must not be rewarded. The architects, primarily left-wing democrats, created laws, took donations, looked the other way, and instead were too busy overseeing donations to their own presidential campaigns and robbing main street blind. Now these same left-wing democrats blame everyone else and get up on their high horses and say, "We are here to save you" from the crises they created.

Chris Wallace was wrong when he said that the McCain-Palin campaign attack on William Ayers is not relevant. Ayers and Obama were financing the radical group ACORN through the organizations that they chaired. ACORN was the main force behind the financial crisis that we now face. It was grassroots socialism from the bottom up rather than the old frame of reference of top-down socialization through government acquisition of areas of production.

According to Frank Pastore, ACORN is involved in election fraud and a number of other things, but in Chicago what Madeline Talbot was doing—and she is actually the person that specializes in doing this—was pressuring financial institutions to make loans to minorities with bad credit ratings and pressuring financial institutions and banks to do this, or else they couldn't merge, or do business, or expand, or whatever, so it was really a smack down. And then what happened is these banks were able then to bundle these and sell them to Fannie Mae. Fannie Mae sold them on the international markets and everything was hunky dory as long as real estate values continued to go up. But if they flatlined or began to turn (as they in fact did), then of course these loans defaulted and you ended up with a $700 billion bailout getting voted on in the House of Representatives.

The New Deal failed to restore economic health, but it did expand the power of government over the people. It was not the usual contest of partisan or bipartisan, republican versus democrat; rather it was more basic. It was the classical republic versus the classical democracy. Government—since the 1910 constitutional amendment to permit the electorate to choose senators directly, rather than through their state legislatures—was becoming less a representative republic than it had once been. It was now being more directly controlled by the people. Voters no longer asked what government was doing on behalf of the general welfare; voters were asking in a very democratic way what the president was doing for them. In his 1961 inaugural address, President John F. Kennedy stated a new approach when he said, "Ask not what your country can do for you, ask what you can do for your country."

As Amity Shlaes points out in *The Forgotten Man*, the real heroes of the day were those people, extraordinary individuals, who embodied the American character by aiding and inspiring their fellow citizens in a variety of innovative ways. Roosevelt claimed that his administration had endeavored to *establish new institutions of public power*, but as usual it was the act of *reconciliation*. One side, the government, gets the power while the other side, the people, gets reconciled to it. Obama seems to be saying, "It's your money, and I want it now."

CHAPTER 20

Religion and the Constitution

With the growing strength of secular humanism and its agenda to instill a dualistic thought process of nature/grace or the divide between fact/value, along with the rise of Darwinism and his naturalistic mechanism for the origin of life, comes the notion that reason is religiously neutral. Secularism and naturalism are falsely promoted as being neutral while biblical views are dismissed as biased private opinions. The desired effect of secular or atheistic humanism is that Christians will abandon the world of ideas and the Christian worldview to the secularists.

It was the Roosevelt administration's goal to transform American politics by creating vast client constituencies who depended on the government for their livelihood. This was first and foremost a philosophical vision, not an economic one. The difference between *original intent* and *limited constitution* of the Founding Fathers and the *living constitution,* which is the ideal of progressives and liberals, was more plainly expressed by Woodrow Wilson when he insisted that "living political constitutions must be Darwinian in structure and practice." The Declaration of Independence affirms that human rights are fixed and unchanging. They are endowed by our Creator and as such are fixed and unchanging, but with a living constitution human rights become historical or evolutionary and are dependent upon government to grant or take away as they see fit to do.

In reading Justice Joseph Story's *Commentaries on the Constitution of the United States*, you will find that the first amendment was enacted for a very narrow purpose and to prohibit a very specific offense.

The founders not only chose not to establish federally any particular denomination of Christianity; they further never intended the first amendment to become a vehicle to promote a pluralism of other religions. As Justice Story explained in his commentaries, "The real object of the First Amendment was not to countenance, much less to advance, Mahometanism, or Judaism, or infidelity, by prostrating Christianity; but to exclude all rivalry among Christian sects."

In reality, Islam must be excluded from any first amendment consideration because in Islam there is no separation of church and state. They are one and the same; there is no separation. Islamic groups openly claim that their goal is not to peaceably assimilate into Western society on equal footing with other religious persons and groups or other religions; they want to dominate completely in all aspects of the culture.

The words of one of the early leaders and founders of this nation serve as a haunting reminder of the need to protect and cherish our Christian heritage and our strength and innocence of character.

Samuel Adams stated, "A general dissolution of principles and manners will more surely overthrow the liberties of America than the whole force of the common enemy. While the people are virtuous they cannot be subdued; but when once they lose their virtue then will be ready to surrender their liberties to the first external or internal invader."

We are at war with Islam and with Shari'ah Law; that is undeniable. Why do academics who teach at the conservative institutions of higher learning continue to destroy the idea of America's Founding Fathers being of strong faith and Christian belief? Michael Babcock PhD, in his book *Unchristian America: Living With faith in a Nation That Was Never Under God*, claims that America has been a four-hundred-year laboratory experiment in living out the humanistic values of the modern age. He discounts the fact that the Founding Fathers invoked God's name in nearly everything they wrote, as described by Dr. Warren Throckmorton of Grove City College.

President Bush and his advisers, one of which was Professor David Forte, held the conviction that Islamic terrorists and Muslim aggressors are, by definition, heretics and not *real* Muslims. Bush and Forte were also proponents of Ecumenical Jihad and shared two fallacies. One is the faulty understanding of Islamic theology which leads them to imagine that *Allah* is more or less interchangeable with the *god* of other monotheists. But as Francis Schaeffer explains, "The Bible is clear: there is a moral law of the universe. And that basic law is the character of God Himself. He is not a contentless God, but a God with a character. His character is the law of the universe. When He reveals this character to us in verbalized, propositional form, we have the commands of God for men. Thus there are absolutes and categories; the law which the God who exists has revealed and which is based upon His character is final. This is the biblical position. The Bible's teaching alone gives moral answers to men."

The line separating good and evil passes not through states, nor between classes, nor between political parties, but right through every human heart and through all human hearts.

CHAPTER 21

─── ⟶ ───

On Becoming a Christian

"I y'am what I y'am and that's all that I y'am" elevated Popeye to philosopher status and makes good sense in a world filled with too many people who say, "Look at me, look at me." Paul's rhetorical skills are never better than when he abstains from using them and boasts of folly and feebleness. In this way, he admonishes us to be a fool for Christ.

"The Christian civilization of the Middle Ages taught European man his own dignity. It taught an emerging Europe a proper respect for individuality, in sharp contrast to Islam." I fear now that they have lost that dignity and strength of character. No one knows what they believe anymore. They don't seem to believe in an afterlife, so where are all of the Christian defenders? I fear that Europe is already lost. Where is a Charlemagne to come from? The new president of France offers hope of a real change in European values.

The Christian idea of vocation, that unique role that each Christian plays in the cosmic drama of creation and redemption, is the one root of the Western idea of individualism. It was not, in its origins, a matter of self-constituting autonomy but of living out the singular, God-given destiny that is every human life.

Moreover, the Christian doctrines of the incarnation (God entering history in the flesh) and the Redemption ("God so loved the world that he gave his only Son...not to condemn the world, but that the world might be saved through him" [John 3:16–17]) gave the world a dignity it could not achieve by its own efforts. Worldliness, in the Christian sense of the term, can have a noble meaning: the core Western conviction about history—that the human story is not just one thing after another—was deeply influenced by Christian doctrine. (Weigel 2005)

Jenny was my daughter, and she was born again in Christ on July 6, 1997. She did not begin her Christian life by faith only to forget it later; she lived by faith each and every moment of her life. She fulfilled the theme of the Christian message set forth by Paul in his letter to Romans. Jenny heard the positive call of salvation, through justification she learned how to become a Christian, and through living the Christian life she gained sanctification and revival. Now her heavenly Father has called her home to receive glorification through eternal life and praise for a job well done.

This is an excerpt from my post on September 6, 2006, "A Life Pleasing God." Jenny and I were members of one of the largest churches in the United States and have been since 1990. I am still a member and active in Adult Bible Fellowships. It is hardly a church of one, and our need to have a personal relationship with God is paramount. Her baptism and profession of faith on July 6, 1997, was the proudest day of my life. We were both active in the deaf and disabilities ministries. I was born again in Christ, in the same manner, many years ago. Our resident in polemics for the forum seems desirous of painting a dark view of my character. So if you wish to look into some of my other postings, my faith in the one true God is always there.

Every believer should desire to know the will of God for their life. He has a specific will and a plan for each of His children.

Ephesians 1:1–14 illustrates this. The will of God has two aspects. He has a determined will and a desired will. The first concerns what He will do; the second concerns what He wants to be accomplished. God's determined will is carried out daily. His desired will includes His general moral laws for all of us and His specific desires for each one of us.

Individualism, as opposed to collectivism, is the concept that all values, rights, and duties originate in individuals. It goes without saying that all men are created equal, that they are endowed by their Creator with certain unalienable rights, that among these are life, liberty, and the pursuit of happiness. These values, rights, and duties are part of man's soul, and at the time of creation God infuses each individual soul directly. I am not speaking of free-thinker-type individuals, where parents feel their children should be allowed to grow up and make that decision for themselves. It takes leadership and strength of character from parents to show them that there is only one way to know God, and that is through Jesus Christ as their Lord and Redeemer.

It is a scandal of American Protestantism that no one knows whether Reinhold Niebuhr did or did not believe in the afterlife taught by Jesus. Look through his writings and you won't find a clear answer. Even his wife did not know or would not tell.

Today, you will not be able to find, or at least you will have a difficult time discovering what any prominent Christian believes. At best they are lukewarm, indifferent to dogmas. General Peter Pace knows what he believes and expressed it clearly. Read Revelation 3:14–22 and Jesus's message, "Listen to what the Spirit says to the churches."

Faith is the supernatural virtue which is *necessary* for salvation. It is a *free gift* of God and is accessible to all who humbly seek it. The act of faith is a *human act*; that is, an act of the intellect of a person— prompted by the will moved by God—who freely assents to divine truth. Faith is also certain because it is founded on the Word of God; it *works* "through charity" (Galatians 5:6); and it *continually grows* through listening to the Word of God and through prayer. It is, even now, a *foretaste* of the joys of heaven.

Though faith is above reason, there can never be a contradiction between faith and science because both originate in God. It is God Himself who gives to us the light both of reason and of faith.

"I believe, in order to understand; and I understand, the better to believe" (Saint Augustine).

The Apostles' Creed

I believe in God, the Father almighty,
Creator of heaven and earth.
And in Jesus Christ, His only Son,
our Lord, Who was conceived by the Holy Spirit,
born of the Virgin Mary,
suffered under Pontius Pilate,
was crucified, died, and was buried.
He descended into hell; the third day
He rose again from the dead;
He ascended into heaven, and sits at
the right hand of God the Father
almighty, from thence He shall come
to judge the living and the dead.
I believe in the Holy Spirit,
the holy Catholic Church,
the communion of saints,
the forgiveness of sins,
the resurrection of the body
and life everlasting.
Amen.

No question about what they believed. The church was spread by these individuals who knew what they believed. They were not afraid to express what they believed, and the Spirit would guide them. There were many disagreements among them, but once again the Holy Spirit would guide them.

God eventually judges all evil. Peter writes about mockers in the last days who sarcastically insist that nothing has changed and that Christ will never sit on His throne of judgment. God is not slow about His promises, but merely patient. Although He seems to withhold judgment, in time we will stand before Him and give an account of ourselves and our actions.

I wonder where Christianity would be today if Martin Luther had not nailed his ninety-five theses to the door of the Wittenberg Church. Luther himself saw the Reformation as something far more important than a revolt against ecclesiastical abuses. He believed it was a fight for the gospel. At the heart of the gospel, in Luther's estimation, was the doctrine of justification by faith—the teaching that Christ's own righteousness is imputed to those who believe, and on that ground alone, they are accepted by God.

CHAPTER 22

Atheistic Humanism

In the history of ideas, it is well known that bad ideas can have lethal consequences. At the heart of the darkness inside the great midtwentieth-century tyrannies were these expressions of atheistic humanism, communism, fascism, Nazism. Henri de Lubac discerned the lethal effects of the marriage between modern technology and the culture-shaping ideas borne by atheistic humanism. "It is not true, as is sometimes said, that man cannot organize the world without God. What is true is that without God, he can only organize it against man."

As stated earlier, all of these tyrannies were expressions of atheistic humanism, and they received their impetus from the *positivism* of Auguste Comte (empirical science is humanity's only reliable tutor), subjectivism, and the materialism of Marx. The main tenet of these philosophies is that only phenomena are knowable as received by the external senses. This leaves no room for such phenomena as moral experiences or introspection.

Progressive education is socialism in its most malevolent and destructive form. It is a form of atheistic humanism in that it is devoid of the necessary moral introspection. It is without that moral clarification that changes the whole view of life. It is evil, and it will destroy Christianity and democracy as it tears away at the very fabric of our constitution, which is based upon Christian principles. "Man's chief end is to glorify God and to enjoy Him forever."

There is a dilemma that we, in a free society, face when black and white is not clear and varying shades of gray appear to isolate the black and white. Finding moral clarity becomes far more difficult. It is very easy for those of us living in a free society to lose moral clarity. In the collective society, the primary challenge is finding the inner strength to confront evil. In the free world, the primary challenge is finding the moral clarity to see evil.

As Amity Shlaes points out in *The Forgotten Man*, the real heroes of the day were those people, extraordinary individuals, who embodied the American character by aiding and inspiring their fellow citizens in a variety of innovative ways. Roosevelt claimed that his administration had endeavored to "establish new institutions of public power," but as usual it was the act of *reconciliation*. One side, the government, gets the power while the other side, the people, gets reconciled to it.

Obama and Reid seem to be saying, "It's your money, and I want it now."

Our national character did not just happen; it developed over time from the beginning of those who braved a long and treacherous ocean voyage seeking religious freedom. The Puritans brought with them the *dream of religious freedom* and the uniquely American ideals of liberty, equality, and democracy, defined in the Declaration of Independence as life, liberty, and the pursuit of happiness, which are unalienable rights endowed by their Creator. It is the very heart and soul of what America was to become. It was the emergence of the national character, our American character.

REFERENCES

Adorno, Theodor W. 1950. *The Authoritarian Personality*. New York, N.Y.

Barton, David. 1999. *Original Intent: The Courts, the Constitution, & Religion.* Aledo, Texas: WallBuilder Press, Coral Ridge Ministries Edition. 7–14.

Burns, James MacGregor. 1963. *The Deadlock of Democracy, Four-Party Politics in America.* Englewood Cliffs, N.J. Prentice-Hall, Inc. Spectrum Edition. 18–23.

Carson, D. A. 2008. *Christ and Culture Revisited.* Grand Rapids, Michigan: Wm. B. Eerdmans Publishing Co.

Coulter, Ann. 2006. *Godless: The Church of Liberalism.* New York, N.Y. Crown Forum, A Division of Random House. 202.

Cottrell, Robert C. 2000. *Roger Nash Baldwin and the American Civil Liberties Union.* New York, NY: Columbia University Press. 32–33.

Croly, Herbert. 1911. *The Promise of American Life.* New York: Macmillan.

D'Souza, Dinesh. 2007. *The Enemy at Home, The Cultural Left and Its Responsibility for 9/11.* New York, N. Y. Doubleday. 184–185.

Evans, M. Stanton. 2007. *Blacklisted by History: The Untold Story of Senator Joseph McCarthy.* New York, N.Y. Crown Publishing, A Division of Random House.

Evans, M. Stanton. 1994. *The Theme is Freedom.* Washington D.C. Regnery Publishing Inc.

Gerlernter, David. 2007. *Americanism: The Fourth Great Western Religion.* New York: Doubleday, a Division of Random House.

147

Goldberg, Jonah. 2007. *Liberal Fascism: The Secret History of the American Left from Mussolini to the Politics of Meaning.* New York, N.Y. Doubleday Publishing Group.

Hofstadter, Richard. 1965. *The Paranoid Style in American Politics.* New York, N. Y. Alfred A. Knopf. 675–6.

The marriage of liberalism and psychology reference to T. W. Adorno and *The Authoritarian Personality*

Hofstadter, Richard. 1981. *The Age of Reform from Bryan to F.D.R.* New York, N.Y. Alfred A. Knopf. 270.

War has always been the nemesis of liberal traditions in America. Ibid., pp. 9–10

Ibid., pp. 204–208 reference: Lincoln Steffans *"Shame of the Cities"* transmuted ethos of responsibility into a sense of guilt and placed blame for the ugly state of affairs on readers.

Hofstadter, Richard. 1964. *Anti-Intellectualism in American Life.* New York, N.Y. Alfred A. Knopf. 145–

Horowitz, David. 1998. *The Politics of Bad Faith.* New York, N.Y. Simon and Schuster. 82–88.

Horowitz, David and Richard Poe. 2006. *The Shadow Party, How George Soros, Hillary Clinton, and Sixties Radicals Seized Control of the Democratic Party.* Nashville, Tennessee Nelson Current, Division of Nelson Communications, Inc. Thomas Nelson, Inc.

Horowitz, David. 2004. *Unholy Alliance.* Washington D.C. Regnery Publishing Inc. 103, 198–199, 240–241.

Kazin, Michael. 2006. *A Godly Hero: The Life of William Jennings Bryan.* New York N.Y. Alfred A. Knopf division of Random House. 225.

Klein, Edward. 2005. *The Truth About Hillary.* New York, NY: Penguin Books. 126–127.

Larson, Edward J. 1997. *Summer for the Gods.* New York, N.Y. Basic Books, Perseus Books.

Lawrence, T. E. 2005. *In War and Peace: An Anthology of the Military Writings of Lawrence of Arabia.* London Greenhill Books Stackpole Books Pennsylvania. 142–147.

Ledeen, Michael A. 2000. *Tocqueville on American Character.* New York, NY: St. Martin's Press. 44–45.

Link, Arthur S. 1960. *Wilson: Volume III, The Struggle for Neutrality 1914–1915.* Princeton, New Jersey Princeton University Press.

Link, Arthur S. 1947. *Wilson: Volume I, The Road to the White House.* Princeton, New Jersey: Princeton University Press.

Link, Arthur S. 1956. *Wilson: Volume II, The New Freedom.* Princeton, New Jersey: Princeton University Press.

Link, Arthur S. 1964. *Wilson: Volume IV, Confusions and Crises, 1915–1916.* Princeton, New Jersey: Princeton University Press.

Link, Arthur S. 1965. *Wilson: Volume V, Campaigns for Progressivism and Peace, 1916–1917.* Princeton, New Jersey: Princeton University Press.

Needleman, Jacob. 2002. *The American Soul, Rediscovering the Wisdom of the Founders.* New York, NY 10014 Penguin Group U.S.A. 12–13, 112–113, 139–144, 112–113, 350–351.

O'Beirne, Kate. 2006. *Women Who Make the World Worse.* New York, NY: Penguin Group U.S.A.

Ring, Kevin A. 2004. *Scalia Dissents, Writings of the Supreme Court's Wittiest, Most Outspoken Justice.* Washington D.C. Regnery Publishing Inc., An Eagle Publishing Co. 280–281.

Shlaes, Amity. 2007. *The Forgotten Man: A New History of the Great Depression.* New York, N.Y. Harper Collins Publishers.

Spencer, Robert. 2006. *The Truth about Muhammad, Founder of the World's Most Intolerant Religion.* Washington D.C. Regnery Publishing, Inc. 102.

Trifkovic, Serge. 2002. *The Sword of the Prophet, Islam history, theology, impact on the world.* Boston, MA: Regina Orthodox Press. 11–12, 26–28.

Tuchman, Barbara A. 1971. *Stilwell and the American Experience in China.*

Tuchman, Barbara A. 1988. *The Guns of August.* The History Book Club. Original publication: 1962.

Weaver, Richard. 1968. *The Southern Tradition at Bay.* New Rochelle, NY: Arlington House. 59–62

Weigel, George. 2005. *The Cube and the Cathedral.* New York: Basic Books. 37–42.

Woods, Thomas Jr. E. PhD. 2005. *How the Catholic Church Built Western Civilization*. Washington, D.C., Regnery Publishing, Inc. 120–121, 105–106, 98, 100–107.

ABOUT THE AUTHOR

———— ✑ ————

The author is a native of Louisville, Kentucky, born and raised. His best friend was named Joe, and they seemed to be adventurers in the world of everything going on around them. The author grew up in a time when the seemingly insurmountable walls were being challenged and breeched. Edmund Hillary conquered Everest, Roger Bannister ran the first four-minute mile, and Shane became the source of much speculation as to where he came from and where he was going after he killed all of the bad guys. They both went to Louisville Male High School. Joe was a year ahead of the author, so the former went to study civil engineering and the author thought that he would follow. He soon found that he should be anything but an engineer, and he eventually ended up in the medical field. While at Male High, he was a classmate of Hunter Thompson. However, they ran in different circles.

The author's interest became pulmonary medicine, and he went into the field of respiratory therapy. He was director of respiratory services at a local hospital, and later on he worked on the Jarvick 7 mechanical heart program. Secretly they all wanted to be Hemingway and lead the life of adventure that he led. Writing was always a part of the author's life, but he did not get serious until later. He saw the world of faith and freedom that he grew up in falling apart around him, and he realized that a lot of people wanted America to fail. That is what this book is about.